UNDERSTANDING

the Doctrine of

GOD'S TIME

OTHER BOOKS BY C. ROBERT LINE

Pure Before Thee: Becoming Cleansed and Changed by Christ

UNDERSTANDING
the Doctrine of
GOD'S TIME

C. ROBERT LINE, PHD

Covenant Communications, Inc.

Printed in the United States of America
First Printing: August 2015

21 20 19 18 17 16 15   10 9 8 7 6 5 4 3 2

ISBN 978-1-68047-664-4

To Andra, Megan, Kyle, Lauren, and McKenna

Contents

For now we see through a glass, darkly; but then face to face: now I know in part; but then shall I know even as also I am known.
—1 Corinthians 13:12

Greater appreciation for the greater universe will also help us to live more righteously in our own tiny universes of daily life. Likewise, a better understanding of God's governance of the vast galaxies can lead to our better self-governance.
—Elder Neal A. Maxwell[1]

---

1 Brigham Young University, 13 August 2002.

Preface

IN RECENT YEARS THERE HAS been a proliferation of stories, books, and movies that, in one way or another, deal with the theme of the perception of time. Some have dealt with time travel or the warping of space-time through interstellar travel. Others have focused on the relativity of time or its relative passage during dreams or dream-induced states of mind. Audiences have not only flocked to see shows on this topic but have become enamored with futuristic possibilities and applications of scientific notions that stretch the imagination and challenge our current perceptions about the world around us. There is a fascination, to say the least, with the theme of time. Whether one is a particle physicist or a cinematic junkie, there seems to be at every level of humanity a desire, even a thirst, to find the meaning of and our place in this baffling concept we call time.

Latter-day scriptures, fortunately, are not silent on the issue of time. To the contrary, prophets ancient and modern, as we will see herein, have commented on and taught various empowering principles relating to time. That's what this book is about—time. It's all about time. It really is. Time is everything, and if we are not careful, we will run out it. Yet there is time and to spare for us to do all that we were sent here to do. "And behold, I, the

Lord, declare unto you, and my words are sure and shall not fail, that they shall obtain it. But all things must come to pass in their time." (Doctrine and Covenants 64:31–32)

Time heals the pain. Well, at least that's what some people say. But does it really? Do we choose the time in which we live? There are those who say they wish they were born in another time. Speaking of the trials he was destined to endure, the fictional Hobbit lamented his lot. "I wish it need not have happened in my time," said Frodo. "So do I," said Gandalf, "and so do all who live to see such times. But that is not for them to decide. All we have to decide is what to do with the time that is given us."[2] And so it goes.

Our existence is defined by time or the lack thereof. Time is what we have every day until it is gone. "Time, unlike some material things," said Elder Maxwell, "cannot be recycled."[3] Time is the great governor of human emotions. This is to say that time can, within the context of our lives, facilitate in us emotions such as anxiety, depression, longing, fear, excitement, joy, anticipation, impatience, and even boredom. It is almost as if we are uncomfortable in (or even allergic to) this realm we call time. In a certain sense we are like a fish out of water—we exist in a realm foreign to our spirits. As Elder Neal A. Maxwell perceptively observed, "Time is clearly not our natural dimension. Thus it is that we are never really at home in time. Alternately, we find ourselves impatiently wishing to hasten the passage of time or to hold back the dawn. We can do neither, of course. Whereas the bird is at home in the air, we are clearly not at home in time—because we belong to eternity. Time, as much as any one thing, whispers to us that we are strangers here. If time were natural to us, why is it that we have so many clocks and wear wristwatches?"[4]

---

2 J.R.R. Tolkien, The Fellowship of the Ring.

3 The Neal A. Maxwell Quote Book, 348.

4 Neal A. Maxwell, devotional address given at Brigham Young University on 27 November 1979.

Time waits for no one, therefore, we must use our time wisely. It is fleeting. Mother Teresa observed, "Yesterday is gone. Tomorrow has not yet come. We have only today. Let us begin." Time flies when you are having fun, they say, but why is that so? Time is money. But which is more valuable, money or time? Time is relative. At least that's what the physicists say. The philosophers say time doesn't even exist. It's an illusion, they claim. As a believer, I am intrigued with the fact that time "is measured only unto man" (Alma 40:8). Therefore God must experience time very differently than we do. We must explore that concept for sure. This book is all about time, though it will take some time to say everything that needs to be said. But don't worry. We have time.

In this book we will discuss three different aspects of time: First, the concept of God's time and its impact on agency and other vital doctrines of the gospel of Jesus Christ. Secondly, we will discuss the nature and importance of time in this temporal existence; including what prophets, ancient and modern, have said about the wise use of time. We will discuss God's timing in our lives and the need to accept the time the Lord has allotted us to live, to work, and to go through trials. Finally, we will briefly explore some doctrines and principles related to the meaning and reality of eternity. This book is a personal endeavor and is not intended to represent the official teachings of the Church of Jesus Christ of Latter-day Saints.

SECTION 1

"All Is As One Day with God": Reflections on God's Time

God's Time and Its Relationship to Agency and the Foreknowledge of God

---

"A thousand years in thy sight are but as yesterday."
(Psalms 90:4)

MANY YEARS AGO I WAS working as a new, full-time seminary teacher of ninth-grade students. One morning, as I was preparing for a class that was to begin within minutes, a loud knock came at my office door. I opened it, and there stood one of my seminary students from the class. I said hello with a smile, but I could immediately tell she was in no mood for pleasantries. I asked her what was wrong.

"Brother Line, my life has no meaning. It isn't worth living!" she exclaimed, her whitened countenance filled with fear and panic.

"Whoa, now . . . what's going on?" I asked. She was one of my best students. She possessed a great attitude about life and had a strong testimony. Because of all this, her distress and anxiety were perplexing to me yet intriguing as well.

"You are to blame Brother Line. You are to blame. It's your fault!" Well, now she had my full attention. "The other day in class you taught us about God and what He is like." We had been in a scripture block the day before where we had highlighted some of Heavenly Father's divine attributes and characteristics. Once again, she lamented, "Oh, my life is over!"

"What on earth did you hear me teach that has you feeling this way?" I asked her as I mentally scanned through an outline of my lesson, searching for anything that could have bothered her so.

"You told us God knows all things, that He is om . . . omni . . ." She was searching for the word we had used and defined in class.

"Omniscient?" I asked.

"Yes. That's it. God is omniscient; He is all knowing . . . Oh, my life has no meaning."

How in the world had this sweet, tender young lady gotten so worked up over a single doctrine that was scripturally sound and doctrinally true?

As a religious educator I have often been confronted with and looked forward to questions from students who are honestly perplexed over doctrinal issues. The "need to know" creates a wonderful climate in which effective teaching and learning can occur. It is thrilling to help students discover that, often, their seemingly difficult and complex questions can be answered in the scriptures in simple and straightforward ways. One such doctrinal issue that has frequently come up in class is the relationship between the doctrine of God's omniscience and its impact on individual agency. There is often an erroneous leap of logic which occurs in the minds of some students, including this young lady's, which goes something like this: "Since God is omniscient, He knows all things, including what I am going to do, even before I do it; therefore there is nothing I can do to change the outcome. I really have no choice. My fate is sealed."

This kind of thinking is not only false (in this case it was borderline acceptance of predestination), but it is also detrimental to attitudes and behaviors (fatalism and the abuse of agency). Sadly, these misunderstandings are sometimes the result of prior teachings dispensed by well-intentioned albeit misinformed instructors. An extensive, well-rounded gospel experience is key to detecting misinformation. In order to truly understand a doctrine, it is vitally important to study that doctrine within the context of related doctrines that provide insight in a complementary fashion. Studying interconnected doctrines can aid us with difficult doctrinal questions.

Do Not Isolate Doctrines—The Gospel-Hobby Key Dilemma

Religious education is a rewarding yet daunting undertaking. There is so much to teach in so little time. It takes thoughtful preparation and hard work to continually teach in edifying and inspiring ways, and learning to rely on the Spirit takes a sustained effort and lots of time. There are so many areas of knowledge to be touched upon, so many doctrines and principles to master. There are historical and cultural considerations to be learned and placed in proper context. Gospel teachers are usually very aware of the need to study all facets of the gospel so as to obtain a well-balanced reservoir of knowledge. Whether intentionally or not, some teachers forget how important it is to have a broad knowledge from which to draw in teaching the doctrines of the gospel so that students may truly understand. Comparing this broad understanding of gospel knowledge to a piano keyboard, Elder Packer gave this warning:

> Some members of the Church who should know better pick out a hobby key or two and tap them incessantly, to the irritation of those around them. By doing this they can dull their own spiritual sensitivities. They can thus lose track of the inspired knowledge that there is a fulness of the gospel and can become, individually, as many churches have become: they may reject the fulness in preference to a favorite note. As this preference becomes exaggerated and distorted, they are led away into apostasy.[5]

---

5 Boyd K. Packer, The Things of the Soul [Salt Lake City, Utah: Bookcraft, 1996].

Elder Packer further observed how this applies specifically to the scriptures: "Instruction vital to our salvation is not hidden in an obscure verse or phrase in the scriptures. To the contrary, essential truths are repeated over and over again. . . . every verse, whether oft quoted or obscure, must be measured against other verses. There are complementary and tempering teachings in the scriptures which bring a balanced knowledge of truth."[6]

Elder Neal A. Maxwell stressed that a well-rounded knowledge of the gospel must include checks-and-balances:

> The system by which the gospel principles are woven together in a fabric . . . keeps them in check and in balance with each other. You see, the doctrines of Jesus Christ by themselves are dangerous. *Any principle of the gospel, isolated, spun off, and practiced in solitude goes wild and goes mad.* It is only the orthodoxy of the gospel that keeps it together, because these are powerful principles that need each other. Just as the people of the Church need each other, *the doctrines of the Church need each other.*[7]

As stated, one such example of a doctrine (if not tempered by other doctrines) that could go "wild and mad" if isolated from the grand picture of things, is the doctrine of God's omniscience. It is certainly true doctrine (see 2 Nephi 2:24; 1 Nephi 9:6; Moroni 7:22; D&C 38:2; Alma 26:35), but it is doctrine that can only be fully understood in the context of other doctrines.

God's Omniscience

Often, when the subject of God's omniscience is brought up, I like to take my classes through a little philosophical conundrum. It goes like this:

"Does God know all things?" To which the class will overwhelmingly answer, "Yes."

6 Boyd K. Packer, "The Pattern of Our Parentage," *Ensign*, Nov. 1984, 66.
7 Neal A. Maxwell, "Charge to Religious Educators," 96; emphasis added.

"Does He know what you will do before you do it?" Now they become a little squeamish, but with a little coaxing the answer, again, is "Yes . . ."

"Does He know what kingdom of glory you will go to?" This one stops them in their tracks. Suddenly they become deeply introspective, but again, they usually answer yes. Then I cuff them with this query: "Is there anything you can do to change what God already knows will happen to you?" Now they are completely baffled. Most do not know what to say, so they usually remain silent. I have to admit it's a little funny to watch them squirm. I stop them before they answer.

"Let me tell you something. I've actually set a trap for you: If you say, 'Yes, there is something I can do to change what God already knows,' then you are saying that God does not know all things, and that is a path we cannot pursue. On the other hand, if you say, 'No, there is nothing I can do, absolutely nothing!' then the danger is that you are on your way to buying in to the false doctrine of predestination and one step away from concluding that we do not have agency after all.

At this point I explain what Elder Maxwell taught about the danger of studying doctrines in isolation. "We have just done this," I explain. Without guiding them through a dissertation on early Christian history, I further note that this is where many theologians of the past went wrong: St. Augustine, Luther, Calvin, etc. I then make the point that, in order to understand the doctrine of God's omniscience, there's a doctrine we need to couple it with—the doctrine or concept of God's time. When we study these two doctrines together, we come to understand that we really do have agency. Let's examine God's time and how it relates to God's omniscience and our agency.

God's Time

In the book of Alma we get a glimpse as to the nature of God's time: "Now whether there is more than one time appointed for men to rise it mattereth not; for all do not die at once, and this mattereth not; all is as one day with God, and *time only is measured unto men*" (Alma 40:8; emphasis added). This teaching is further amplified by Doctrine and Covenants 130:6–7: "The angels do not reside on a planet like this earth; but they reside in the presence of God, on a globe like a sea of glass and fire, where *all things for their glory are manifest, past, present, and future, and are continually before the Lord*" (emphasis added). Similarly, Joseph Smith taught: "The great Jehovah contemplated the whole of the events connected with the earth, pertaining to the plan of salvation, before it rolled into existence, or ever 'the morning stars sang together' for joy; *the past, the present, and the future were and are, with him, one eternal 'now'*."[8] In short, God experiences time differently than we do. We live in the present. The past is done and gone. And the future is yet to be. But somehow, in a way we do not fully comprehend, God lives in the past, present, and future all at once. His reality of time comprises all three states at the same time. In fact, in a manner of speaking, God exists outside of what we know as linear time. So Alma is not only correct but also precise in saying that "time is only measured unto man"!

Although we may not be able to fully comprehend this state of timelessness in which God lives, we can look to several metaphors and scientific notions that help us come to a better understanding of this peculiar state. Renowned physicist Albert Einstein postulated the well-known theory of relativity, which, among other things, offers an interesting perspective on the concept of time. Einstein argued that the faster a person travels, the slower the passage of time relative to someone who is stationary. With travel on earth, if we compare someone traveling on an airplane to someone who's stationary, for example, the difference in the passage of time for both does indeed occur, but the difference is minuscule. However, an astronaut traveling through space at extremely high velocities for lengthy periods of time would discover when he returned to earth a significant difference in the way he's experienced time compared to his

8 *Teachings of the Prophet Joseph Smith*, 220; emphasis added.

counterparts on earth. He would find that everyone on earth had aged significantly more than he had on his long, interstellar voyage.

The fastest speed known in the universe is a particle, or wave, of light. Light travels extremely fast—over 186,000 miles per second. We are nowhere close to building airplanes or spacecraft that can go this fast, but if we could build such a craft, it could circumnavigate the globe eight times in one second. That's how fast light travels! Another way to look at the speed that light travels is to contemplate the distance from our earth to the sun, which is ninety-three million miles. When we look at the sun in the middle of the day (not a wise thing to do for very long, I might add), we are not actually looking at the sun the way it looks presently. We are actually seeing what the sun looked like approximately eight minutes earlier. This is because it takes light traveling from the sun eight minutes to travel ninety-three million miles at the speed of light!

As said before, we are nowhere close to reaching the speed of light in space travel. Einstein argued that, in reality, no one could ever go this fast due to the fact that as you get closer and closer to reaching the speed of light, your mass increases (you become increasingly heavier) and one could never carry enough rocket fuel to push on to those greater speeds. However in theory, if we were able to attain to the speed of light, according to Einstein's theory embodied in the famous equation of special relativity ($E=mc^2$), two things would happen. First, an individual's mass (m) would become infinite, and second, time would slow down and eventually stop. Past, present, and future would all be one! In light of all this (no pun intended) it is interesting to note that God is a being of light—for Him past, present, and future are all one. Hopefully we will know more one day how all these theories fit together with God's eternal laws, yet the correlations we are finding with science and scripture as they relate to God's time are absolutely fascinating. What we can say for sure is that time is relative both from a scientific perspective and a scriptural perspective. In the

Doctrine and Covenants, Joseph Smith addresses this concept: "In answer to the question—Is not the reckoning of God's time, angel's time, prophet's time, and man's time, according to the planet on which they reside? I answer, Yes." (D&C130:4–5).

Here's another approach to understanding God's time. Many years ago, Lael Woodbury, dean of the College of Fine Arts and Communications at Brigham Young University, spoke in a CES fireside about man's perception of time and God's perception of time in these words:

> The evidence suggests that God . . . perceives time as we perceive space. That's why 'all things are before him, and all things are round about him; and he is above all things, and in all things, and is through all things, and is round about all things' [D&C 88:41]. Time, like space, is 'continually before the Lord.' . . . Right now we perceive music in time as a blind man perceives form in space—sequentially. He explores with his fingers, noting form, texture, contours, rhythms. He holds each perception in his mind, one by one, carefully adding one to the other, until he synthesizes his concept of what that space object must be like. You and I don't do that. We perceive a space object immediately. We simply look at it, and to a certain degree we 'know it. We do [not] go through a one-by-one, sequential, additive process. We perceive that it is, and we are able to distinguish it from any other object. . . . I'm suggesting that God perceives time as instantaneously as we perceive space. For us, time is difficult. Lacking higher facility, we are as blind about time as a sightless man is about space. We perceive time in the same way that we perceive music—sequentially.

We explore rhythm, pitch, amplitude, texture, theme, harmonies, parallels, and contrasts. And from our perceptions we synthesize our concept of the object or event—the musical artwork—that existed in its entirety before we began our examination of it. Equally complete now is each of our lives before the Lord. We explore them sequentially because we are time-blind. But the Lord, perceiving time as space, sees us as we are, not as we are becoming. We are, for him, beings without time. We are continually before him—the totality of our psyches, personalities, bodies, choices, and behaviors.[9]

Also in regard to God's seeing the totality of our existence at once, Neal A. Maxwell observed: "God does not live in the dimension of time as do we. We are not only hampered by our finiteness (experiential and intellectual), but also by being in the dimension of time. Moreover, God, since 'all things are present' with him, is not simply predicting based solely on the past. In ways that are not clear to us, he sees rather than foresees the future, because all things are at once present before him."[10]

Elder Maxwell's statement highlights an interesting dilemma we sometimes fall into. We often answer the question "Why does God know what you are going to do before you do it?" with something like this: "It's because He is sort of like a parent. Because He knows your personality so well, has seen you make so many other choices, He just has a really good idea of what you will choose. He's a really good guesser." However, as logical as this appears, it contradicts the scriptures and living prophets. Elder Maxwell's statement helps us to see that God is not guessing, nor predicting, nor anticipating what we will do.

---

9 "Continually before the Lord, Commissioner's Lecture Series" [Provo: Brigham Young University Press, 1974], 5–6.

10 Maxwell, *Things As They Really Are*, 29.

"He sees, rather than foresees" because all things (past, present, and future) are continually before Him.

Once the doctrine of God's time is understood (not that we grasp it experientially), we can then begin to more fully understand things about God's omniscience. The fact of the matter is this. God knows what we are going to do beforehand not because He knows us so well (which He does, but as an explanation it still leads to predestination); rather, He knows what we will do before we do it because from His perspective, His dimension relative to time (and in ways which we will never fully comprehend in this life), He has already seen us make the choice!

This is a vital doctrine in many respects. For one thing, it refutes the Socinianistic notion that God's omniscience is limited to "necessary truth" (meaning that which will *definitely* happen in the future) while rejecting the idea that His omniscience does not apply to "contingent truth" (meaning that which *may* happen in the future). This argument is advanced by some due to a limited view (and thus judgment) of God. They assert that we still have our agency because God only knows of the things that will definitely happen but not the things that "may" happen, like what choices we will make. Socianists would say that if God knew every possible future event, human free will would be untenable. While this has a nice, logical appeal, it is, nonetheless, incongruent with scripture: "O how great the holiness of our God! For *he knoweth all things, and there is not anything save he knows it*" (2 Nephi 9:20; emphasis added). Likewise, we are told that "the Lord knoweth all things *which are to come*" (Words of Mormon 1:7). "All" apparently means *all* things—past, present, and future. To Abraham the Lord declared: "I know the end from the beginning" (Abraham 2:8).

We do have full agency, and God does have full, or complete, omniscience. Scriptures concerning the doctrine of God's time help us understand that the reality of God's complete omniscience does not preclude the real exercise of agency. In fact, there are several latter-day scriptures that mention these two interrelated doctrines together in an apparent cause-and-effect relationship: "And I have a work for thee, Moses, my son; and thou art in the similitude of mine Only Begotten; and mine Only Begotten is and shall be the Savior, for he is full of grace and truth; but there is no God beside me, *and all things are present with me, for I know them all,*" (Moses 1:6). Also this verse from the Doctrine and Covenants: "The same which *knoweth all things*, for *all things are present* before mine eyes" (D&C 38:2). The implication is that it's only because God lives outside of linear time that He is able to know all things. It seems reasonable to reverse engineer the scripture this way: If past, present, and future were not all "present" with God, He wouldn't be able to know all things. It appears that both of the aforementioned scriptures make God's omniscience a function of the particular state, relative to time, in which He dwells. As it says in the Book of Mormon, "Except he was a god he could not know of all things" (Helaman 9:41).

Additionally, in these two scriptures we see the doctrines of omniscience and of God's time taught together in an interconnected fashion. We can take two doctrines that "need" each other and use them to learn truths we could not arrive at if we viewed them separately. In trigonometry, if we know the measure of two angles and the length of one line segment of a triangle, and, if we know how to do the math, then we can also ascertain the measure of the third angle, the lengths of the other two lines, the area, the perimeter, and the height of the triangle. Spiritually speaking, it is the same. With a few basic pieces of information (like two basic doctrines, such as God's time and omniscience) we can come to a higher knowledge. Alma calls this gaining "the greater portion of the word" (see Alma 12:10). These aren't things we're merely hypothesizing about. They are simple truths, much like mathematic formulations, that can be discovered when certain facts are combined. Thus, in our discussion of these two doctrines, a student can "do the math" and see how we can have both omniscience and agency.

How an Understanding God's Time Helps Us to Better Understand Other Doctrines

"Time makes more converts than reason."
—*Thomas Paine*

SOME MIGHT ARGUE THAT A concept such as God's time is not particularly significant to our salvation and therefore not worthy of our time and attention. The fact remains, however, that God's time is an element of scriptural truth reinforced repeatedly in all the standard works of the Church. So, why is God making scriptural mention of His frame of time? Understanding the fact that God knows everything because He sees everything all at once can positively impact the way we understand other doctrines of the gospel as well.

For instance, concerning the lost 116 pages of the Book of Mormon (see D&C 3, 10), a perplexing question arises: How did the Lord know, centuries before, the necessity of having Nephi create a near-duplicate record that one day would replace (or restore) the 116-page manuscript that would become lost? Nephi didn't know why he was including it, but the Lord did. The Lord *knew* what would happen. He knew that the 116 pages would become lost. Was there a possibility Joseph and Martin would not lose those pages? Not a chance, because the Lord was not *predicting* what would happen. It was not because

He knew Martin's and Joseph's weaknesses so well but because of His perspective (His time). He saw the mistake already made and was thus able to provide the duplicate record. Thus it is that "the works, and the designs, and the purposes of God cannot be frustrated, neither can they come to naught. For God doth not walk in crooked paths, neither doth he turn to the right hand nor to the left, neither doth he vary from that which he hath said, therefore his paths arc straight, and his course is one eternal round. Remember, remember that it is not the work of God that is frustrated, but the work of men" (D&C 3:1–3). Understanding God's time can have a positive impact indeed on how we see and understand a variety of other doctrinal themes, including and especially those significant to our salvation.

God's Time and the Doctrine of Creation

The doctrine of God's time is also valuable when discussing the doctrine of the Creation. However, we should first consider an aspect of the interrelated doctrine of the Fall. In 2 Nephi 2:21, we learn that because of Adam's transgression his "time was lengthened," perhaps suggesting that linear time as we know it did not exist before the Fall. This notion is strengthened in Abraham 5:13: "But of the tree of knowledge of good and evil, thou shalt not eat of it; for *in the time* that thou eatest thereof, thou shalt surely die. Now I, Abraham, saw that *it was after the Lord's time*, which was after the time of Kolob; *for as yet the Gods had not appointed unto Adam his reckoning*" (emphasis added). These scriptures both suggest that mortal time as we know it not only commenced with the Fall of Adam but that conditions in the Garden of Eden (and during the periods of creation) were after "the Lord's time," where past, present, and future are all one. Although it's hard for us to wrap our finite minds around that actual concept, when one considers its ramifications, there are new perspectives that become apparent with the process of creation.

Often teachers and students of the gospel debate about the "length of time" of the Creation. A biblical literalist would claim it took six days. Some Latter-day Saints incorrectly argue that it took six thousand years, since each day for God is a thousand years on earth.[11] Some individuals use the book of Abraham (see chapter 4) to argue that there were six indefinite time periods all called "days," concluding that a "day" of creation could be millions of years or more. Students who lean toward the theory of evolution rather than toward creationism often find this approach appealing. However, if the Creation occurred before mortal time (as we know it) was instituted, none of these approaches has merit. Why? Because all deal in one way or another with linear time. When we consider that the Creation occurred in God's time, we realize that evolutionary claims of science, along with discussions of dinosaurs, plate tectonics, million year ages and epochs, etc., need not dissuade us from believing in the Creation account. Nor do we need to feel any unjustified, dogmatic allegiance to our interpretation of the Creation and thus be dismissive of evolutionary claims. We need not worry. Though we do not understand all concerning the Creation, nor will we until the Second Coming (see D&C 101:32-34), the idea of *God's time* being in play before the Fall opens up a myriad of possibilities.

Perhaps the term *days* is used in the Creation accounts as a device given by God to man so that he might form some sort of rudimentary metric by which to envision the complexities of those things that are unexplainable because of the timeless dimension in which God resides. The first two verses of Doctrine and Covenants 29:31-33 explain: "For by the power of my Spirit created I them; yea, all things both spiritual and temporal—First spiritual, secondly temporal, which is the *beginning* of my work;

---

11 The problem with this approach is clarified in the Pearl of Great Price, where we learn that a thousand years on earth is as one day, *not with God, but on Kolob,* which is "nigh" (meaning near) unto God (see Abraham 3:1–12). This is to say that time is relative. As one gets closer to the presence of God, time slows down until it stops and past, present, and future all become one. This is not only sound doctrine, but remember Einstein? It has scientific roots as well.

and again, first temporal, and secondly spiritual, which is the *last* of my work" (emphasis added). From these verses we learn the simple truth that all things are first created spiritually, then temporally (or physically). This is precisely what we are taught in Moses 3:5, wherein the Lord states: "For I, the Lord God, created all things, of which I have spoken, spiritually, before they were naturally upon the face of the earth." However, according to Doctrine and Covenants 29, this process is just the "beginning" of God's creative work. Verse 32 clarifies that God takes those "temporal," or physical, creations and creates them spiritually again. This is described as being the "last" of God's work. This does not mean that all things created, including mankind, will ultimately end up as spirit again. There is a difference between "being a spirit" and "being a spiritual being." To become a spiritual being is the process of coming to earth, where our spirits are first clothed in an earthly or physical body and then undergo the process of being "born again," as Christ taught Nicodemus, "by water and the spirit" thus putting off the natural man.[12] Now that we think we are beginning to understand things a bit, we read D&C 29:33: "Speaking unto you *that you may naturally understand*; but unto myself *my works have no end*, neither beginning; but it is given unto you that ye may understand, because ye have asked it of me and are agreed." It is as though

---

12 Furthermore, we one day will die and temporarily lose our physical body but then become resurrected with a perfected body of flesh and bone but without blood. Instead we will have a spiritual substance flowing through our bodies. We will finally be glorified, resurrected, spiritual beings. In Doctrine and Covenants 88 we read how the earth will be sanctified and quickened, or resurrected, and how "the righteous [you and I] shall inherit it. For notwithstanding they [you and I] die, they also shall rise again, a *spiritual body*" (vv. 25–27; emphasis added). The fact of the matter is that God is not done creating us; He intends to complete the process, thus fulfilling His work and glory to bring to pass the immortality and eternal life of man (see Moses 1:39) and thus making us "spiritual beings" like He is—glorified, resurrected beings!

the carpet has been pulled out from under us! After describing to us the full process of creation, the Lord in essence says: "Actually, that's not quite how it happened. I'm just giving you a basic framework of principles you can understand in the time-bound realm in which you live. Actually, there is no beginning or end to the creative work." We stand all amazed. Once again, being part of this linear-time-bound existence, there are certain things we simply will not comprehend while we are here. Though we do not now fully grasp the concept of God's time, He nevertheless gives us glimpses into this doctrine in the scriptures so we can get by. He simply asks us to study and pray, to have the faith to accept things as they are, to realize that His ways are higher than ours (see Isa. 55), and to "Believe in [Him]; believe that he is, and that he created all things, both in heaven and in earth; believe that he has all wisdom, and all power, both in heaven and in earth; believe that man doth not comprehend all the things which the Lord can comprehend" (Mosiah 4:9).

God's Time and the Atonement

Understanding the issue of God's time likewise gives meaning to the doctrine of the Atonement, specifically the suffering Christ endured for the sins of humanity in Gethsemane. Often we are prone to think of the Savior having a "moment" of mass suffering for all sins all at once. As we learn from the scriptures, though, Christ suffered for more than just sin (see Alma 7:11–12). He experienced, in ways we do not fully comprehend, all our pains, heartaches, trials, joys, and successes. In short, He can fully comprehend all of our emotions and experiences because He has experienced them all vicariously. It is difficult to understand in terms of linear time how this could be. However, when one considers the ramifications of God's time, where past, present, and future are all present, we begin to at least slightly fathom how Christ might possibly have been able to experience not just a massive amount suffering all at once but also what we each experience individually. Illustratively, Elder Merrill J. Bateman once said:

For many years I envisioned the Garden of Gethsemane and the cross as places where an infinite mass of sin and pain were heaped upon the Savior. Thanks to Alma and Abinadi, it is no longer an infinite mass but an infinite stream of people with whom the Savior became intimately acquainted as he suffered our sins, pains, and afflictions. I testify that he knows each of us, is concerned about our progress, and has the infinite capacity not only to heal our wounds but also to lift us up to the Father as sanctified sons and daughters.[13]

Could it be that Christ not only suffered an infinite atonement but that He suffered it infinitely—meaning of course, not in linear time but in God's time (see D&C 19:1–12)? Thinking of the Atonement in this perspective helps us to make sense of certain scriptures that might otherwise be confusing, for example:

For behold, the time cometh, and is not far distant, that with power, the Lord Omnipotent who reigneth, *who was, and is from all eternity to all eternity*, shall come down from heaven among the children of men, and shall dwell in a tabernacle of clay, and shall go forth amongst men, working mighty miracles, such as healing the sick, raising the dead, causing the lame to walk, the blind to receive their sight, and the deaf to hear, and curing all manner of diseases." (Mosiah 3:5; emphasis added)

"For behold he judgeth, and his judgment is just; and the infant perisheth not that dieth in his infancy; but men drink damnation to their own souls except they humble themselves and become as little children, and believe that *salvation was, and*

---

13 3 Sept 1996, "A Peculiar Treasure."

is, and *is to come*, in and through the atoning blood of Christ, the Lord Omnipotent." (Mosiah 3:18; emphasis added).

> "And I have a work for thee, Moses, my son; and thou art in the similitude of mine Only Begotten; and mine *Only Begotten is and shall be the Savior*, for he is full of grace and truth; but there is no God beside me, and *all things are present with me, for I know them all.*" (Moses 1:6; emphasis added)

Of particular interest is this next scripture from the Pearl of Great Price, where the Lord is conversing with the prophet Enoch thousands of years before the Savior performed His great atoning sacrifice. Notice the verb tense here: "And behold, Enoch saw the day of the coming of the Son of Man, even in the flesh; and his soul rejoiced, saying: *The Righteous is lifted up, and the Lamb is slain from the foundation* of the world; and through faith I am in the bosom of the Father, and behold, Zion is with me" (Moses 7:47; emphasis added). It is as though the Atonement was not only operative thousands of years before Christ but also already accomplished (see Alma 39, chapter heading). How could this be the case if the Atonement were not performed somehow outside of linear time? (See also Mosiah 4:6-7; Mosiah 3:13; Jarom 1:11, and Mosiah 16:6)

Not only does this perspective help us to gain a greater grasp of the possible operational aspects of the Atonement, but it gives us a greater personal appreciation for it as well. Indeed, the emphasis on salvation as an individualized function rather than as a group function is emphasized in the words of scripture, ancient and modern. President Howard W. Hunter observed:

> I have always been impressed that the Lord deals with us personally, individually. We do many things in groups in the Church, and we need organizations of some size to allow us to administer

the Church well, but so many of the important
things—the most important things— are done
individually. We bless babies one at a time, even if
they are twins or triplets. We baptize and confirm
children one at a time. We take the sacrament,
are ordained to the priesthood, or move through
the ordinances of the temple as individuals—as
one person developing a relationship with our
Father in Heaven. There may be others nearby
us in these experiences, just as there are others in
your classroom, but heaven's emphasis is on each
individual, on every single person.[14]

Similarly, C. S. Lewis observed: "God is not hurried along
in the Time-stream of this universe any more than an author is
hurried along in the imaginary time of his own novel. He has
infinite attention to spare for each one of us. He does not have
to deal with us in the mass. You are as much alone with Him as
if you were the only being He had ever created. When Christ
died, He died for you individually just as much as if you had
been the only man in the world."[15]

God's Time and the Second Coming

The scriptures are replete with references to the fact that no
one knows the time of the Second Coming (see D&C 39:21;
D&C 49:7; D&C 51:20; D&C 61:38; D&C 130:14-16; D&C
133:11; see also Joseph Smith–Matthew 1:38-48). Joseph Smith
taught: "Jesus Christ never did reveal to any man the precise
time that He would come. Go and read the Scriptures, and you
cannot find anything that specifies the exact hour He would
come; and all that say so are false teachers."[16] Some suggest that
the reason we do not know when He will come is because it's not

---

14 CES Fireside, 10 February 1989.

15 *Mere Christianity*, 168.

16 *Teachings of the Prophet Joseph Smith*, 341.

up to God to decide when He will come, it's up to us. They assert that perhaps when we get our act together as individuals and as a Church, then Christ will come. This may sound compelling and reasonable, but such conjecture has inherent flaws. Elder McConkie's statement seems to put such speculation to rest: "As to the Second Coming, the time is fixed, the hour is set, and, speaking after the manner of the Lord, the day is soon to be. The appointed day can be neither advanced nor delayed. It will come at the decreed moment, chosen before the foundations of the earth were laid, and it can be neither hastened by righteousness nor put off by wickedness. It will be with our Lord's return as it was with his birth to Mary: the time of each coming was fixed by the Father."[17]

Additionally, the parable of the ten virgins, wherein five of the virgins are ready and five are not, seems to be inconsistent with the notion of a flexible date or time for the Second Coming. Both President Kimball and Elder Bednar assert that the ten virgins represent the members of the Church. In light of this we might conclude that some Church members will not be prepared at the time of the Second Coming, or by a certain date.

On the other hand, seeming to support the belief that it depends on when we get our acts together, President Kimball offers: "If the members of the Church do real proselyting in their home wards . . . the number of converts could grow to astronomical figures and *even hasten the time when the Lord will be returning* to the earth in His second advent."[18] Similarly, Brigham Young taught: "The length of time required 'to accomplish all things pertaining to Zion' is strictly up to us and how we live, for creating Zion commences in the heart of each person."[19] President Young also said, "If the people neglect their duty, turn away from the holy commandments which God has given us,

17 *New Witness of the Articles of Faith,* 591.
18 Spencer W. Kimball, Conference Report, Oct. 1976, 4.
19 *Journal of Discourses,* 9:283.

seek their own individual wealth, and neglect the interest of the kingdom of God, we may expect to be here quite a time—perhaps a period that will be far longer than we anticipate."[20]

Now, which view is right? Well, maybe both are. From our perspective, it is up to us to "hasten the day"; that is, it hasn't been decided yet *from our perspective*. However, from God's perspective and time the issue has been decided. The day is fixed, and why? Because, once again, He sees past, present, and future. It is all before Him. He certainly knows when the Second Coming is going to occur, and not because He is good at guessing, but because, from His perspective, He has already seen the exact day it will occur.

The Nature of God

We are told in scripture that God "is not a partial God, *neither a changeable being;* but *he is unchangeable from all eternity to all* eternity" (Moroni 8:18), and that "from eternity to eternity *he is the same,* and his years never fail" (D&C 76:4). So how do we reconcile that with this famous statement that follows? President Lorenzo Snow, speaking of a doctrinal insight he perhaps learned from Joseph Smith in a sermon he gave at the funeral of King Follet, said "As man now is, God once was; as God is now man may be."[21] Well, which is it? Is God that same unchangeable being from eternity to eternity, or was He once a mortal like us and then became a God, as we may become? The answer is yes and yes! The fact of the matter is that once God became God, He always was God—that same unchangeable being from eternity to eternity. Here again, the doctrine of God's time provides insight. When Heavenly Father was resurrected and attained His godlike state, past, present, and future all became one for Him. In His godlike state, mortal time frames were no longer separate in linear sequence but eternal, in unchanging existence. In essence, God became Himself, His eternal self. Once he passed from a

---

20 *Journal of Discourses,* 11:102.
21 *The Teachings of Lorenzo Snow,* ed. Clyde J. Williams [1984], 1.

realm of linear time to timelessness, it was as though He had always been a God, since His past, present, and future became an eternal now. Likewise, when we are resurrected as exalted beings like He is, we too will always have been gods!

Another interesting aspect of God's nature has to do with the geography of His existence. We are told in Doctrine and Covenants 88:41 that God "comprehended all things, and all things are before him, and all things are round about him; and he is above all things, and in all things, and is through all things, and is round about all things; and all things are by him, and of him, even God, forever and ever." We know God is omniscient (all knowing) and that He is omnipotent (all powerful). Likewise, God is omnipresent, perhaps in ways that go beyond just the influence of His Spirit being felt. Remember, in his theory of relativity Einstein postulated that if an individual were to reach the speed of light, not only would time stop, but an individual's mass (represented as "m" in $E=mc^2$) would become *infinite*. In essence, that individual would be everywhere at once. How all this applies to God being omnipresent and in timelessness we do not know, but it seems like Einstein was on to something.

Prophetic Visions

It is bothersome to certain individuals that the events in certain prophetic visions (i.e., the books of Ezekiel, Revelations, and Isaiah, etc.) are not always sequential. However, it should come as no surprise that prophets like Isaiah and John the Revelator jump all around time frames in their narratives because, as *seers*, they are "seeing" through the eyes of God. Perhaps they are telling their stories through the process of themes rather than sequence or chronology. Prophets back then were not predicting nor necessarily foretelling today's future social conditions. They were literally seeing our day, along with all the needs we would have as Church members, family members, and as members of the human race. A "seer is a revelator and a prophet also" (Mosiah 8:15–16), but a seer is able to "see," albeit in limited, permissible, and needed ways, through the lens and perspective of God's time, where all things are past, present, and future.

Prayer

How does God listen to and answer all of our prayers at once? I will defer to C. S. Lewis and his wise and insightful statement on this matter:

> A man put it to me by saying "I can believe in God all right, but what I cannot swallow is the idea of Him attending to several hundred million human beings who are all addressing Him at the same moment." . . .
>
> Now, the first thing to notice is that the whole sting of it comes in the words *at the same moment*. Most of us can imagine God attending to any number of applicants if only they came one by one and He had an endless time to do it in. So what is really at the back of this difficulty is the idea of God having to fit too many things into one moment of time.
>
> . . . Our life comes to us moment by moment. One moment disappears before the next comes along: and there is room for very little in each. That is what Time is like. And of course you and I tend to take it for granted that this Time series—this arrangement of past, present and future--is not simply the way life comes to us but the way all things really exist. We tend to assume that the whole universe and God Himself are always moving on from past to future just as we do.
>
> God is not in Time. His life does not consist of moments following one another. If a million people are praying to Him at ten-thirty tonight,

He need not listen to them all in that one little snippet which we call ten-thirty. Ten-thirty—and every other moment from the beginning of the world—is always the Present for Him. . . . He has all eternity in which to listen to the split second of prayer put up by a pilot as his plane crashes in flames.[22]

We can certainly see based on Lewis's explanation how the doctrines of God's omniscience, of His time, and of prayer are complementary. When taken out of context, it's hard to fathom how God could attend to so many of our petitions all the time, but given the big picture, it starts to make sense.

Conclusion

Though we will likely never grasp the concept of God's time while here in mortality, there is a reason for God's scriptural utterances regarding this doctrine. Perhaps we are given temporal glimpses of eternal realities that we might cope in our limited, linear existence. Nonetheless, there is much we can learn as we view some of the gospel's pivotal doctrines through this fascinating lens.

---

22 "Time and Beyond Time," *Mere Christianity.*

Time after Time: The Redemption of the Universe and the Operation of the Atonement on Other Worlds

"All men must see that the teaching of religion by rules and rote is largely a hoax. The proper teaching is recognized with ease. You can know it without fail because it awakens within you that sensation which tells you this is something you've always known."
— *Frank Herbert*[23]

SEVERAL YEARS AGO I TAUGHT an evening institute class on the Pearl of Great Price. One of the topics we briefly touched on that night was the infinite nature of Christ's Atonement, and specifically, how the effects of the Atonement extend to other worlds created under the direction of Heavenly Father. We were nearing the end of the semester, and the course had gone well. I felt a connection with many of the students, especially one young man who had been a wonderful participant in class discussions. After class, this young man approached me nearly in tears. He was a thoughtful individual with a love for truth and a countenance that radiated the light of the gospel. He was bright, both spiritually and intellectually and was in his first year of medical school at a prestigious university. He asked with meekness and sincerity if I had time for a few questions.

In all my twenty-plus years in Church education, I had never seen a student struggle with what he related to me next.

He told me how pleased he was that we had spent some time, albeit briefly, talking about the infinite Atonement and its operational effects on other earths. He acknowledged he knew (as we had stated in class) that scripturally we didn't know much about this matter. He then told me how, for years, one specific aspect of this topic had bothered him immensely, an aspect he asserted that he had been taught by quite a few other religious educators. He was uncomfortable with the idea of Jesus Christ being the one cosmic savior for all the "millions of earths" created under the direction of the Father and this is not even "a beginning to the number of [His] creations" (Moses 7:30). It didn't seem right to him that out of the millions and billions of His children born on the other millions and billions of other earths, that we were the only ones fortunate enough to have been born on the same earth He came to. The idea did not seem spiritually or doctrinally sound to him. When I asked why he felt so uncomfortable with this, he related to me that such a notion sounded highly improbable from a statistical standpoint, that of all the billions and billions of earths with inhabitants who are God's children, Christ just so happened to born on this earth and not on any of those other earths. Statistically it was the probability that bothered him, that is to say, he felt such odds of this occurring (one earth out of billions and billions) were so low, so remote, that the whole idea seemed implausible to him. He had a testimony of Christ and the Restoration of the gospel, but he felt that this one-cosmic-savior teaching was troublesome and even a bit preposterous.

He was shocked when I empathized with him and confessed that I'd had the very same question and concern for years. We then spoke for over an hour, and I shared some scriptural verses and some personal insights. Although we never fully answered his questions, he said with a smile as we concluded that night, "I am so relieved. I think I can let this question go now." Some of what I shared with him now follows.

The Cosmic Question of Salvation

The Book of Mormon clearly and consistently asserts that the Atonement of Jesus Christ is an infinite Atonement (see 2 Nephi 9:7; 25:12; Alma 34:9-14). As Elder Nelson has explained, it is infinite in a variety of ways: "His Atonement is infinite . . . in that all humankind would be saved from never-ending death. It was infinite in terms of His immense suffering. It was infinite in time, putting an end to the preceding prototype of animal sacrifice. It was infinite in scope—it was to be done once for all."[24]

Additionally, the Atonement appears to be infinite in the sense that it applies to other worlds. We are informed in latter-day scripture that "by him [Christ], and through him, and of him, the *worlds* are and were created, and *the inhabitants thereof* are *begotten sons and daughters unto God*" (D&C 76:24; emphasis added). *Begotten* in this sense appears to mean "spiritually begotten" through the Atonement, as evidenced in Mosiah 5:7: "And now, because of the covenant which ye have made ye shall be called the children of Christ, his sons, and his daughters; for behold, this day *he hath spiritually begotten you*; for ye say that your hearts are changed through faith on his name; therefore, ye are born of him and have become his sons and his daughters" (emphasis added). To be sure, we know that Heavenly Father, not Jesus, is the Father of our spirits in a literal sense. However, Jesus Christ is referred to often in the scriptures as "Father" in the sense that He is the father of our spiritually reborn selves. Through faith, repentance, baptism, and the reception of the Holy Ghost, we are "born again," so to speak, through the power of the infinite Atonement.

The infinite power of the Atonement not only affects Heavenly Father's spirit children on this world, but it is also available and efficacious for each of Heavenly Father's children on other worlds, "yea, millions of earths like this," and this is "not [even] a beginning to the number of [His] creations."

---

24 See also Tad R. Callister, *The Infinite Atonement,*

Elder Nelson confirmed this by saying that "the mercy of the Atonement extends not only to an infinite number of people, but also *to an infinite number of worlds.*"[25] Similarly, Elder Bruce R. McConkie stated, "When the prophets speak of an infinite Atonement, they mean just that. Its effects cover all men, the earth itself and all forms of life thereon, and reach out into the endless expanses of eternity. . . . the Atonement of Christ, being literally and truly infinite, applies to an infinite number of earths"[26]

Occasionally the question is raised, as it was by my student, whether or not Christ (the man Jesus Himself) is *the one* redeemer of each and every world as well. For certain, the power of the Atonement is operative on each of these worlds, but who facilitates that power? Illustratively, the rooms in a house may all be lit up, but what is the source of the light? Is it just one lamp, or are several lamps contributing to that light? Furthermore, each room may have its own source light, but one single source (i.e., the sun) can be sufficient to light up each room at midday. Though the "power" of the Atonement is infinite and always present throughout time and space, it could be that there is a Savior who puts that power into operation for His specific earth. The power to redeem is always there, but it is activated by the one who makes the sacrifice, one having the keys over death and hell, much like the keys and power of the priesthood always exist, but they are activated by each prophet who holds the mantle to use them. More will be said on this topic in a latter chapter regarding the operational effects of the Atonement in the premortal existence and extending through the eternities.

This question regarding the operation of the effects of the Atonement on others worlds might possibly be answered in a single verse of scripture: "But only an account of this earth, and the inhabitants thereof, give I unto you" (Moses 1:35). The answer to the question we are seeking is elusive. The

25 "The Atonement," *Ensign*, Nov. 1996, 35.
26 *Mormon Doctrine*, 64–65.

revealed word is scanty, if not mute, on the matter. Elder Neal A. Maxwell's words are instructive on this point: "As to the Lord's continuing role amid His vast creations, so little has been revealed. There are [only] inklings"[27]—fragments, if you will, that appear in the scriptural record, so as to make any declaration about these matters tenuous at best. We know that the power of the Atonement is operative in other worlds, and we know that the specific man, even Jesus Christ, is our Savior here on *this* earth. But beyond this the scriptures do not speak. Personal interpretations can be made, speculations can be proffered, and seemingly convincing assertions can be spoken, but to say more than this is opinion only.

Thus, to travel further on this point, we must leave the plain (and preferred) scriptural record and rely alone on opinion, theory, and assumption. However, before traveling out into uncharted waters, we would do well to remember these words from President Harold B. Lee: "All that we teach in this Church ought to be couched in the scriptures. . . . If you want to measure truth, measure it by the four standard Church works. . . . If it is not in the standard works, you may well assume that it is speculation . . . and if it contradicts what is in the scriptures, you may know by that same token that it is not true. This is the standard by which you measure all truth."[28] The First Presidency said the following regarding the importance of the standard works on May 4, 2007:

> Not every statement made by a Church leader, past or present, necessarily constitutes doctrine. A single statement made by a single leader on a single occasion often represents a personal, though well-considered, opinion, but is not meant to be officially binding for the whole Church. With

---

27 Neal A. Maxwell, "Our Creator's Cosmos," CES Conference 13 August 2003.

28 *The Teachings of Harold B. Lee*, 148–49.

divine inspiration, the First Presidency . . . and
the Quorum of the Twelve Apostles . . . counsel
together to establish doctrine that is consistently
proclaimed in official Church publications.
This doctrine resides in the four "standard
works" of scripture (the Holy Bible, the Book of
Mormon, the Doctrine and Covenants, and the
Pearl of Great Price), official declarations and
proclamations, and the Articles of Faith. Isolated
statements are often taken out of context, leaving
their original meaning distorted."[29]

Thus, as we begin our travels here, we recognize that what
follows is not a declaration of doctrine but an exploration of
doctrinal ideas. We realize that where there is no scriptural
concurrence, we are sailing solely on the winds of conjecture.
Hopefully, we will attempt to drop anchor, as we are permitted,
in ports that at least have some semblance of scriptural support.
The purpose in this particular journey is not to find doctrinal
land, since that has not been made available to us at present,
but to wade through the currents and splash around a little,
if you will, hopefully finding the most reasonable channels
through which we can safely navigate.

Viewpoint #1—One Galactic, Cosmic, Universal Savior

One viewpoint holds that the very person known as Jesus
Christ, the Savior of *this* world, is the *one* Savior for *all* the
worlds ever created, "yea, millions of earths like this," which
are not even "a beginning to the number of" earths that ever
were or ever will be created under the direction of Heavenly
Father (Moses 7:30). This notion has a few adherents who also
interpret scripture to say that the resurrected Christ actually
went and visited these other earths and ministered personally
to them (see D&C 88:51–61; 3 Nephi 16:1–3).

---

29 LDS Newsroom, "Approaching Mormon Doctrine," lds.org.

A statement by President Marion G. Romney is often cited as support for this camp of thought: "Jesus Christ, in the sense of being its Creator and Redeemer, is the Lord of the whole universe. Except for his mortal ministry accomplished on this earth, his service and relationship to other worlds and their inhabitants are the same as his service and relationship to this earth and its inhabitants. In short, Jesus Christ, through whom God created the universe, was chosen to put into operation throughout the universe Elohim's great plan 'to bring to pass the immortality and eternal life of man'—the gospel of Jesus Christ—the only way whereby man can obtain eternal life."[30] Although this particular viewpoint lacks any conclusive and clear support from canonized scripture, there is one verse often cited as supporting it: "After the many testimonies which have been given of him, this is the testimony, last of all, which we give of him. That he lives! For we saw him, even on the right hand of God; and we heard the voice bearing record that he is the Only Begotten of the Father That by him, and through him, and of him, the worlds are and were created, and the inhabitants thereof are begotten sons and daughters unto God" (D&C 76:24).

A little more than a decade later, Joseph Smith prepared a poetic version of the vision recorded in Doctrine and Covenants 76, part of which recasts verse 24 as follows: "And I heard a great voice, bearing record from heav'n. He's the Savior, and only begotten of God. By him, of him, and through him, the worlds were all made, Even all that careen in the heavens so broad, Whose inhabitants, too, from the first to the last, Are sav'd by the very same Savior as ours; And, of course, are begotten God's daughters and sons, By the very same truths, and the very same pow'rs." This poetic version, it could be argued, is just as vague as the scriptural version; neither clearly says what those who quote it hopes it says. One camp interprets

30 Marion G. Romney, "Jesus Christ: Lord of the Universe," *Improvement Era*, Nov. 1968, 46, 48.

"the very same Savior as ours" to mean *the* Christ who came to this earth, while the other camp feels that "the very same Savior as ours" is comparative, meaning "exactly the same *type* of Savior." Illustratively, there may be a child who complains at dinnertime that he wants a different slice of pepperoni pizza from the box (from whence all slices are cut equally the same and all have pepperoni) than the one on his plate. His parent replies, "The slice on your plate is *very same* slice as that which is found in the box; just as are those slices your brothers and sisters are eating currently and have already eaten and will yet eat!" Does the term "very same" mean "specifically" the same slice of pizza, or might it mean the same "type" pizza slice?

Before moving on, we should take a moment to summarize the apparent strengths and weakness of the viewpoint that Christ is *the* Savior for all worlds. The merits include, but are not limited to, the following: First,

1. For some individuals (though certainly not all—like the student I mentioned earlier) it is humbling to realize how fortunate we are to be born on *the very* earth Jesus was born on, rather than on any one of a billion or so other earths where he was not born. This would seem to indicate a favored, or at least, fortunate status for every earthly inhabitant.

2. The power of the Atonement is made more potent since we can seemingly center our faith better on just one Savior and not many. This reflects a desire to avoid any religious stance that would be in any way polytheistic.

Here are some thoughts as to why this approach may not work so well:

1. It's not explicitly taught in the scriptures. Even if we were to rely on this camp's interpretation of D&C 76:24 (which tends to be the only scripture ever referenced in support of this point of view), it must be remembered that truth is not established by one witness but by several harmonizing with one another. Remember, Elder Packer taught that "instruction vital

to our salvation *is not hidden in an obscure verse* or phrase in the scriptures" and that *"essential truths are repeated over and over again.* Every verse, whether oft-quoted or obscure, *must be measured against other verses.* There are complementary and tempering teachings in the scriptures which bring a balanced knowledge of truth."[31] Conversely, there are many verses that *do* support the idea of multiple saviors, which we will examine hereafter.

2. There is a cosmic complexity that exists in regard to redemption of worlds and their associated inhabitants that would make this model unfeasible. We are told in scripture that other worlds have been redeemed by the power of the Atonement, even before our earth, and that many more earth's will yet be created and redeemed: "For behold, there are *many worlds that have passed away* by the word of my power.[32] And there are many that now stand . . . and as one earth shall pass away, and the heavens thereof even so shall another come; and there is no end to my works" (Moses 1:35–38). It seems unlikely that there would be people on other worlds, perhaps billions of worlds before ours, who lived through their earth's life cycle and saw their earths become celestialized through the power of the Atonement long before the one galactic, cosmic

---

31 *Ensign,* Nov. 1984, 66; emphasis added.

32 The phrase "word of my power" in context of this chapter refers to Christ, or the Only Begotten Son (see Moses 1:32). So to say that a "world passes away by the word of my power" is to say that all earth's, like ours, are ultimately redeemed by the Atonement of Jesus Christ. Joseph Fielding Smith said: "This earth is a living body. It is true to the law given it . . . this earth is living and must die . . . the earth, as a living body, will have to die and be resurrected, for it, too, has been redeemed by the blood of Jesus Christ" (*Doctrines of Salvation,* 1:72–74).

Savior would ever be born on our earth.[33] Many are familiar
with the statement made by Lorenzo Snow: "As man is God
once was, and as God is man may become." This simple yet
sublime couplet has staggering implications. Rodney Turner, a
former BYU professor of religion, made this observation:

> In drawing aside the curtains of eternity and
> revealing the multiplicity of interrelated gods,
> lords, fathers, mothers, kings, queens, sons and
> daughters who make up a celestial cavalcade
> stretching forever backward and forever forward
> along the intersecting highways of endless time,
> the Prophet Joseph Smith demolished once and
> for all those confining doctrines concerning the
> Creator and his creations. Just as Copernicus
> overturned the myopic medieval notion of a
> Ptolemaic physical universe in which the sun,
> moon, and stars revolved in obeisance around
> this one tiny planet, so did Joseph Smith destroy

---

33 One thoughtful observer has noted that it seems evident in the scriptures that any earth and its associated inhabitants "cannot be saved without its dead (D&C 128:18), and ordinance work for the dead must be
completed before a world passes away (since it must be done by mortals),
and until Jesus entered the spirit world and bridged the gap between
the righteous and the unrighteous there could be no ordinance work for
the dead (*Doctrines of Salvation*, 1:128), nor could Christ resurrect until
after he gained a resurrected body (Ibid.), yet many former worlds passed
away to their glory long before Christ established ordinance work for the
dead, and before he gained power to resurrect. Some have suggested that
perhaps the departed from these former worlds waited in the spirit world
until Jesus instituted ordinance work for the dead (and rose with power
to resurrect), but if they did it would have been too late to save them, for
their worlds had already passed away leaving no mortals to do their work!
And are we not told that the one-third who rebelled in heaven were cast
down to THIS earth (Rev. 12), and that we who came to THIS earth
to gain a body, etc., constitute the other two-thirds who kept their first
estate." (Samuel Wattles, September 2008)

the equally myopic notion of a lone triune deity creating and sustaining all things throughout the boundless reaches of absolute space. When the Prophet Joseph Smith revealed that the true theological universe really was Copernican in nature, the Latter-day Saints were freed from the traditional scriptural strait-jacket worn by most Christians. For the fact that there really are "gods many, and lords many" ruling over 'worlds without end' simply will not allow for a theological Ptolemaic universe, a universe that never did, and never will, exist."[34]

So what are we to conclude about the myriad of exalted beings who once lived as mortals? How were they redeemed? Did they have a Savior as well? Was their Savior our Savior? This seems highly unlikely since it would mean that our Heavenly Father (during His sojourn as a mortal) could only be redeemed (from either spiritual and/or physical death) through the Atonement that would be made operative by His Son! And what if, hypothetically speaking, the Son failed? Would Heavenly Father cease to be God?

3. Statistically this view is possible but highly improbable. One can see in this approach shades of the pre-Copernican notion that everything just happens to revolve around the earth. This myopic scientific notion would later prove to be false—the earth wasn't the center of everything; it just appeared that way to a people who not only lacked the truth but were unable, through limited reasoning, to even conceive the truth.

4. There is difficulty in trying to imagine how the gospel would be taught on these other worlds. Any missionary discussion on another earth relating to the birth of the Savior might include

---

34 "The Doctrine of the Firstborn and Only Begotten," in *The Pearl of Great Price: Revelations from God*, ed. H. Donl Peterson and Charles D. Tate Jr. [Provo, UT: Religious Studies Center, Brigham Young University, 1989], 91–118.

these words as prefacing remarks: "A long, long time ago, in a galaxy far, far away . . ."

Once again, these matters have not been fully revealed. As Elder Maxwell stated, there are only minute scriptural inklings on this subject. One of these "inklings" that is often erroneously interpreted is the quasi-scriptural claim that not only is there one galactic, cosmic Savior but that our earth was the only one wicked enough to kill Him. The scriptural word actually says the following: "Wherefore, as I said unto you, it must needs be expedient that Christ—for in the last night the angel spake unto me that this should be his name—should come *among the Jews,* among those who are the more wicked part of the world; and *they shall crucify him*—for thus it behooveth our God, and there is none other *nation* on earth that would crucify their God" (2 Nephi 10:3; emphasis added). In no way does this verse say that our *earth* was the only one wicked enough of all the earths to kill Jesus. Can we safely make an extrapolation from the Jews to the rest of the universe? Where would such an interpretive stretch come from? Consider the following: In his conversation with the prophet Enoch, the Lord declares: "Wherefore, I can stretch forth mine hands and hold *all the creations which I have made*; and mine eye can pierce them also, and *among all the workmanship of mine hands there has not been so great wickedness as among thy brethren*" (Moses 7:36; emphasis added). These two scriptures are not commenting on the same audience—a group unlike any other that would crucify Christ (the Jews) versus a group that is more wicked than any other on earth (Enoch's brethren).

There are no latter-day cross-references between these two verses in the footnotes of our Church-sanctioned scriptures. If such a connection were doctrinally viable, surely an authorized cross-referencing would be made to clarify the doctrinal point. It should be further noted that the phrase "all the creations which I have made" is in the context of Enoch's people, "these thy brethren," in verse 32, rather than *all* of God's creations that have ever been anywhere on any earth in the universe. Thus, this claim of our earth being the only one wicked enough to crucify Christ is not substantiated by scriptural context nor warranted as a doctrinal interpretation.[35]

Viewpoint #2 – Multiple Saviors, One for Each Earth

This viewpoint holds that each world has its own savior, that is to say, a savior for each earth like this earth with inhabitants who are spirit children of one Heavenly Father. This notion claims that, given the fact that there are "millions of earths like this," and they are not even "a beginning to the number of" earths that ever were or ever will be created under the direction of Heavenly Father (Moses 7:30), so likewise there would be just as many corresponding saviors. In support of this point is a statement made by Brigham Young: "Sin is upon every earth that ever was created. Consequently every earth has its redeemer, and every earth has its tempter; and every earth and the people thereof, in their turn and time, receive all that we receive and pass through all the ordeals that we are passing through."[36] What he meant by saying "its redeemer" is not exactly clear. But it seems to indicate there may be multiple saviors. To say that all the worlds and their inhabitants are redeemed by Christ is a true statement. What we do not know

---

35 There is another scripture, a parable found in D&C 88:46-61, often referenced, which, although not exactly matching this first viewpoint, is nonetheless intriguing. I would submit that this parable, though interesting, is ambiguous enough that a discussion or potential interpretation is unwarranted.

36 Journal of Discourses, 14:71-72; Brigham Young also taught the following in *Journal of Discourses*: "There never was any world created and people nor never would be but what would be redeemed by the shedding of the blood of the Saviour of that world." (5/12/1867) Also, "Every world has had an Adam, and an Eve: named so, simply because the first man is always called Adam, and the first woman Eve; and the oldest Son has always had the priviledge of being ordained, appointed and called to be the heir [and] Saviour of [that] family." 10-8-1854 Eliza R. Snow surmised: "Moreover, Jesus is one of a grand order of Saviours. Every world has a distinctive Saviour." (Women of Mormondom).

for sure is whether Christ is a title or the person Himself, or both. Nevertheless, all are redeemed by the Atonement, all are redeemed by Christ. We know that Adam and Eve are not only individuals of this earth but apparently titles as well for the first man and woman on each earth (see Moses 1:34; 4:26).

As to the plausibility of this viewpoint, speaking of Christ's infinite Atonement, Rodney Turner wrote:

> That which is infinite by nature need not be unlimited in scope. Christ's atonement was infinite in that it was an act of God, rather than an act of finite man (2 Nephi 9:7; Alma 34:10; 2:15; D&C 20:17–18). While the Atonement was unquestionably "infinite" or all-encompassing pertaining to everything that fell in consequence of Adam's transgression, it is doubtful if its efficacy was literally boundless. Scripture indicates that the Fall and the Atonement, like the two sides of a coin, are inextricably linked together and co-extensive in their effects (1 Cor. 15:22; 2 Nephi 2:22–26). If so, Jesus' atonement was not infinite in an absolute sense any more than Adam's fall was infinite in an absolute sense. . . . Since the processes of creation, birth, death, resurrection, and salvation were on-going realities eons of time before Jesus came into organized existence, his preeminence must be relative, not absolute. . . . Then too, if there is but one redeemer for all possible worlds, those individuals who achieved godhood prior to Jesus' sacrifice on this earth, or who will attain it in the endless future, were, or will be, dependent for their salvation upon an individual extremely remote from their own time and circumstance."[37]

---

37 In H. Donl Peterson and Charles D. Tate, Jr., eds., *The Pearl of Great Price: Revelations from God*, 100–1.

As mentioned, one of the virtues of this second point of view is the existence of many scriptural verses that, although not necessarily conclusive, at least allow for the possibility of multiple saviors. One such example is found in the book of Moses. While speaking to the Lord and being shown in vision many earths (see Moses 1:29), Moses inquires how these worlds were made. The Lord responds: "And by the *word of my power*, have I created them [each earth], *which is mine Only Begotten Son*, who is full of grace and truth" (v. 32; emphasis added). Although this verse is somewhat vague at first glance, it is apparent that "Only Begotten Son" refers back to "word of my power." We know from John 1 that another name for Christ is "the Word." So *Christ*, or *Only Begotten Son*, here, appears to be synonymous with "the word." In Moses 1:33, the Lord again confirms that He created the myriad earths by the Son: "And worlds without number have I created; and I also created them for mine own purpose; and *by the Son I created them, which is mine Only Begotten [or 'word of my power']*" (emphasis added). Then comes this intriguing declaration, which shows that not only are worlds created by "the word of my power," but that these worlds also "pass away" (meaning they are celestialized; see D&C 77:1; 88:18–27; and 130:6–9) by that very same power, or by the Atonement of Christ: "But only an account of this earth, and the inhabitants thereof, give I unto you. For behold, *there are many worlds* [earths] *that have passed away by the word of my power* [by Christ, or the Atonement]. And there are many that now stand, and innumerable are they unto man; but all things are numbered unto me, for they are mine and I know them."

Thus it is clear that "word," in the context of these verses (32–35) refers to Christ. What follows next, when read in context of the previous verses, is thought provoking: "And the Lord God spake unto Moses, saying: The heavens, they are many, and they cannot be numbered unto man; but they are numbered unto me, for they are mine. And as one earth shall pass away, and the heavens thereof even so shall another come; and there is no end to *my works* [earths], neither to *my words*" (Moses 1:37–38; emphasis added). Now, one could make the assertion that "words" means Heavenly Father speaks a lot. However, based on the scriptures in Moses and 1 John above, we see this in an entirely different context. To be sure, we must avoid a certain and conclusive interpretation, but we can at least see that verse 38 allows for the possibility of multiple saviors (or *words*), one for each earth, as Brigham Young reasoned.

Additionally, in 2 Nephi 9:21 we are informed that Christ "cometh into the world *that he may save all men* if they will hearken unto his voice; for behold, *he suffereth the pains of all* men, yea, the pains of every living creature, both men, women, and children, *who belong to the family of Adam*." The phrase "who belong to the family of Adam" is an inclusive statement which categorizes a finite group. If there really were one galactic, cosmic savior for all the billions and billions of earths that have ever been, such an inclusive phrase would not be needed.

A similar inclusive phrase can be found in the Doctrine and Covenants 76:40–42: "And this is the gospel, the glad tidings, which the voice out of the heavens bore record unto us—That he came into the world, even Jesus, to be crucified for the world, and to bear the sins of the world, and to sanctify the world, and to cleanse it from all unrighteousness; That *through him all might be saved whom the Father had put into his power* and made by him" (emphasis added). One way to look at this is that Christ (the man Jesus who lived on this earth) saves only those souls the Father specifies He (Christ) can and will save. Again, such a phrase would not be necessary if there were just one universal redeemer. One argument against this is found in Doctrine and Covenants 76:1: "Hear, O ye heavens, and give ear, O earth, and rejoice ye inhabitants thereof, for the Lord is God, and *beside him there is no Savior*" (emphasis added), unless this too, is a categorical or inclusive statement, meaning that besides Christ, there is no other Savior for *our earth*. This would be sound reasoning as well and would not necessarily preclude the existence of saviors on other earths.

There are other interesting and noteworthy verses we should mention as well. In the Book of Mormon we are told that Jesus "shall make intercession for *all the children of men*" (2 Nephi 2:9; emphasis added), which could imply that this is not necessarily so for all the children *of God.* Alma tells us, "I was thus racked with torment, while I was harrowed up by the memory of my many sins, behold, I remembered also to have heard my father prophesy unto the people concerning the coming of one Jesus Christ, *a* Son of God, to atone for the sins of the world" (Alma 36:17; see also D&C 3:16). Perhaps this is merely semantics, but perhaps not. If there were indeed one cosmic Christ, it might say *the* Son of God, not "*a* Son of God." Additionally, in Mosiah 4:7, we read: "I say, that this is the man who receiveth salvation, through the atonement *which was prepared* from the foundation of the world *for all mankind, which ever were since the fall of Adam,* or who are, *or who ever shall be, even unto the end of the world.*" Though inclusive, here is yet another insightful statement. As shown by the number of scriptural verses that could support it, the viability of this second perspective seems to be stronger and more logical than the once cosmic savior model.

Viewpoint #3—God's Time Perspective

For the third viewpoint, let's revisit the doctrine and reality of God's time. Remember our small glimpse into the nature of God's time in Alma? We talked about how "all is as one day with God, and time only is measured unto men" (Alma 40:8). We also pointed out that "all things for [our] glory are manifest, past, present, and future, and are continually before the Lord" (D&C 130:6-7). And we added Joseph Smith's assertion that "the past, the present, and the future were and are, with him, one eternal 'now.'"[38]

Thus far we've been examining the notion of the operational effects of the Atonement on other worlds (and throughout endless age of "time") through the perspective of linear time.

---

38 *Teachings of the Prophet Joseph Smith,* 220.

Could it be that neither of the first two viewpoints presented is the reality? If "past" includes "all pasts" and future includes "all futures" to come; and furthermore, if past, present, and future really are "one eternal 'now'" to God, perhaps there is a reality that is in some way a composite of the first two viewpoints or maybe something entirely different altogether. Perhaps we will find that the very question being posed herein is irrelevant!

Perhaps we need to consider, given the reality of God's time and state of being, that "the eye hath never seen, neither hath the ear heard, before, so great and marvelous things" and that "no tongue can speak, neither can there be written by any man . . . so great and marvelous things" as we are contemplating here (3 Nephi 17:16–17). Perhaps the answer to our question is found in an arena of timeless truth that has not "yet entered into the heart [or mind] of man" (D&C 76:10). Surely we are contemplating matters "which surpass all understanding in glory, and in might, and in dominion" and that are "not lawful for man to utter; Neither is man capable to make them known, for they are only to be seen and understood by the power of the Holy Spirit, which God bestows" on those who are properly prepared and have paid the probationary price to know all things (D&C 76:114–16).

Conclusion

Elder Neal A. Maxwell once spoke about the grandeur of the universe, with all its divine creations. In speaking specifically of the immense value LDS theology adds to our understanding of these things, Elder Maxwell said the following:

> The late Carl Sagan, who communicated effectively about science and the universe, perceptively observed that 'In some respects, science has far surpassed religion in delivering awe. How is it that hardly any major religion has looked at science and concluded, 'This is better than we thought!

The Universe is much bigger than our prophets said-grander, more subtle, more elegant. God must be even greater than we dreamed'? Instead, they say. 'No, no, no! My god is a little god, and I want him to stay that way.' A religion, old or new, that stressed the magnificence of the Universe as revealed by modern science *might be able to draw forth reserves of reverence and awe hardly tapped by the conventional faiths.* Sooner or later, such a religion will emerge."[39]

How blessed we are in this latter day for the additional insights we have from the Book of Mormon, Doctrine and Covenants, Pearl of Great Price, and from modern prophets and apostles. We truly stand in awe as we realize that the "heavens, they are many, and they cannot be numbered unto man; but they are numbered unto [God], for they are [His]" (Moses 1:37).

Yet with the great expanse of knowledge the Restoration brings, after all is said and done, it is perhaps safest to rely on the only sure approach to the question at hand: "Only an account of this earth give I unto you" (Moses 1:35).

Perhaps we will one day we will come to envision and understand things we have "never considered" and realities we have "never had supposed" (D&C 101:94; Moses 1:10) But for the present we must patiently remember that "there is not only so much to know but also so much to become, [that] vital truths are not merely accumulated in the mind but are expressed in life as well. . . . As, more and more, we brush against truth, we sense that it has a hierarchy of importance. Some truths are salvationally significant and others are not. . . . It is clear from the verses of scripture that some truths may turn out to have a place in a yet-to-be-revealed hierarchy of truth

39 CES Conference on the Doctrine and Covenants and Church History, 13 August 2002, at Brigham Young University quoting Carl Sagan, *Pale Blue Dot: A Vision of the Human Future in Space*, 50; emphasis added.

which the world doesn't anticipate. . . . One even wonders if truths, like planets, might belong to a particular order."[40]

Yet, while we are becoming, we ponder. We study and strive to attain to "the greater portion of the word" (Alma 12:9-11). And although we are only given an account of this earth and the inhabitants thereof, perhaps that is not only sufficient, perhaps it is the point; we are doing that which is done on other worlds. We are following a grand, eternal pattern, as suggested by Orson Pratt:

> The dealing of God towards his children from the time they are first born in Heaven, through all their successive stages of existence, until they are redeemed, perfected, and made Gods, is a pattern after which all other worlds are dealt with. . . . The creation, fall, and redemption of all future worlds with their inhabitants will be conducted upon the same general plan. . . . The Father of our spirits has only been doing that which His progenitors did before Him. Each succeeding generation of Gods follow the example of the preceding ones. . . . [The same plan of redemption is carried out] by which more ancient worlds have been redeemed. . . . Thus will worlds and systems of worlds . . . be multiplied in endless succession through the infinite depths of boundless space; some telestial, some terrestrial, and some Celestial, differing in their glory."[41]

---

40 Neal A. Maxwell, *Ensign*, April 1993.

41 *The Seer*, "Pre-existence," 134-35.

SECTION 2

"God's Timing": Reflections on Time in
Our Temporal Existence

Precious Time: Prophetic Priorities and Using Time Wisely

If it came down to choosing to go to your child's championship basketball game, attending an important church meeting, or staying late at the office to make sure you met that critical deadline for the big project, which would you choose? Is there a way to know how we should prioritize the many aspects of our lives so we don't have to feel guilty that we are letting others down?

YEARS AGO, WHEN MY WIFE and I were in the first few years of marriage, I had a poignant experience that caused me to deeply reflect on my priorities. I had just come home from work tired and hungry but excited for the big game that would be televised that night. It was starting just as I pulled into the driveway; I was in a hurry to get inside to watch. As I opened the door, my wife greeted me. Although I didn't notice it at the time, she was all dressed up and had done the same with our little two-year-old daughter. Additionally, she had prepared a wonderful dinner with all the trimmings. The house had been cleaned spotlessly, and soft music wafted through the air. To all of this thoughtful preparation I was completely oblivious. She had prepared a wonderful evening simply to express her love for me, as I would painfully soon realize. I quickly gave her a hug, asked in a somewhat casual way how her day had gone, and proceeded to the TV. I loosened my tie, sat back, and began to take in the game. Honestly, it took several minutes before I realized she was still standing near the door where she greeted me, watching me watch the game. I will never forget the disappointment on her face. Although I turned off the game and offered a half-baked apology, the night (though not totally ruined) had been soured by my insensitivity. The worst part of all was when she explained to me she sometimes felt she was number two in my life. I felt ashamed. My heart ached. That evening I silently vowed that somehow, someway, this would never happen again.

My wife knew I really did love her, but my actions had undermined my love and commitment. My experience caused me some serious soul searching and caused me to ask myself many questions. What is our most important priority in life? Is it our Church calling? Is it our spouse or children? Is it our occupation? Frequently our choices in life consist of simple distinctions between good and evil. At other times they do not. Often we find that decision-making is actually fraught with perplexing choices between good versus better, important versus vital, and needful versus essential. Perhaps this dilemma is one of the very reasons we come to this mortal sphere—to experience the interplay between time, talents, and agency. Fortunately, Latter-day prophets and seers have given us clear and ample guidance not only as to what our specific priorities should be but also how we can establish and balance them.

After the conclusion of an Church Educational System (CES) fireside on February 5, 1999, Elder Jeffery R. Holland offered additional counsel to the faculty and guests that remained in the Assembly Hall on Temple Square. Among other things, he gave the following ranking of priorities for our lives: 1) our physical and spiritual selves, 2) our spouses, 3) our children, 4) our Church callings, 5) our professional life, and 6) our civic responsibilities. Elder Holland assured us that this list was nothing new and that prior prophets had taught the same. In 1972, President Harold

B. Lee counseled: "Most men do not set priorities to guide them in allocating their time, and most men forget that *the first priority should be to maintain their own physical and spiritual strength.* Then comes their family, then the Church, and then their professions— and all need time."[42]

Our Spiritual Selves

It may seem perplexing to some to say that our first priority must be self. How can this be, especially when we have been counseled about the importance of family, not to mention the scriptural admonition that invites us to "lose ourselves" in the service of others? In 1994, President Howard W. Hunter gave this counsel: "*Your first obligation is to get your own spiritual life in order* through regular scripture study and daily prayer . . . [you should also] secure and honor your priesthood and temple covenants."[43] Similarly, President Ezra Taft Benson counseled: "To be successful, we must have the Spirit of the Lord. We have been taught that the Spirit will not dwell in unclean tabernacles. Therefore, *one of our first priorities is to make sure our own personal lives are in order.*"[44] As these prophets' teachings infer, putting ourselves first is, in reality, putting God first, or at least our relationship to Him "through regular scripture study and daily prayer," etc. In this way we use our agency, through obedience, to invite the companionship, guidance, and cleansing effects of the Holy Ghost, thus assuring that the power of the Atonement of Jesus Christ is operative in our lives.

"Family first" is a doctrinal declaration of one of our most sublime values. Yet, as Elder Holland and President Lee suggest, our relationship with and obedience to God takes precedence. Elder Russell M. Nelson puts into perspective the relationship

---

42 Bishop's Training Course and Self-Help Guide, sec. 2, p. 7. Also in James E. Faust, "Happiness Is Having a Father Who Cares," Ensign, January 1974, 23; italics added.

43 Howard W. Hunter, Conference Report, October 1994, 69; italics added.

44 Ezra Taft Benson, Come unto Christ, 92.

between this first priority and the next two, mainly, our spouse and children, as follows: "As we go through life even through very rough waters, a father's instinctive impulse to cling tightly to his wife or to his children may not be the best way to accomplish his objective. Instead, if he will lovingly cling to the Savior and the iron rod of the gospel, his family will want to cling to him and to the Savior."[45]

When properly applied, this principle not only allows our loved ones to cling to and love us, but it also allows us to more fully love them. "Only when we love God above all others," taught Elder Marlin K. Jensen, "will we be capable of offering pure, Christlike love to our companions for all eternity."[46]

This placement of priorities is not a self-centered approach to living, as we can see in the Savior's admonition that we lose ourselves for others: "If any man will come after me, let him deny himself, and take up his cross, and follow me. For whosoever will save his life shall lose it: and whosoever will lose his life for my sake shall find it" (Matthew 16:24-25). The Joseph Smith Translation of Matthew 16:26 gives us this clarifying detail: "*And now for a man to take up his cross, is to deny himself all ungodliness, and every worldly lust and keep my commandments.*" To deny ourselves of all ungodliness means we must take appropriate care of our spiritual and physical selves so that we might put of the natural man and become a Saint. The appropriate placing of these things first is, as was said before, putting God first. Losing ourselves is in reality relinquishing *selfishness* and becoming what God would have us be. Elder Neal A. Maxwell gives these clarifying insights:

> Losing oneself means losing concern over getting
> credit; by knowing our true identity we need not be
> concerned about seeming anonymity. . . . Losing
> oneself means yielding the substance of one's

---

45 Russell M. Nelson, Conference Report, October 2001, 84.
46 Marlin K. Jensen, Ensign, October 1994, 46-51.

own agendum if it does not match the agendum
of the Lord. . . . Losing oneself means keeping
ourselves more spiritually intact . . . so that
we are able to help more. . . . Losing ourselves
means being willing to go to Nineveh when we
would much prefer to go to Tarshish . . . Losing
oneself means losing one's impulsiveness. . . .
Losing ourselves means dropping our resistance
to feedback so that we can grow faster, just as did
meek and receptive Moses, the brother of Jared,
Peter, and Joseph Smith.[47]

The Physical and Spiritual Self: A Divine Intermingling

Keeping ourselves "spiritually intact" and putting of the natural
man does not mean that we disregard our physical well-being.
There are those, however, who would discredit and diminish
any attention to the physical, zealously quoting 1 Timothy
4:8, wherein Paul counsels: "For bodily exercise profiteth *little*:
but godliness is profitable unto all things" (emphasis added).
Lest we misunderstand this scripture, the footnote in the LDS
edition of the scriptures points out the Greek translation,
which renders the phrase this way: "Bodily exercise profiteth *a
little while*" (emphasis added). This clarification bears out the
principle that while physical exercise *is* worthwhile, someday
we will all be hindered by the aging process. If we can exercise,
we should.

To say that our spiritual self is our first priority is under-
standable when considering it as a function of placing God
and His commandments above all else. Thus to some it may
appear at odds to elevate one's physical well-being to the same
level. Nevertheless, latter-day revelation declares unequivocally
the importance "of things both temporal and spiritual (1 Nephi

---

47 Neal A. Maxwell, A Wonderful Flood of Light (Salt Lake City, Utah:
Bookcraft, 1990), 99.

15:32)" as regards the mortal soul. "The spirit *and* the body are the soul of man," and "spirit *and* element, *inseparably* connected, receive a fullness of joy; and when separated, man cannot receive a fullness of joy" (D&C 88:15; 93:32-33; see also D&C 45:17; 138:50). Body and spirit are complementary. One who is strong spiritually understands the importance of keeping the body as strong and healthy as possible in order to serve God and man. It is difficult to give to others and serve them when we lack the health and vigor to do so. We are commanded not only to serve God with all our heart and mind, but also with might and strength (D&C 4:2; Moroni 10:32).

Spiritual attainment is a function, in part, of physical mastery. One who would control and expand his spiritual self knows the importance of controlling the physical self. President Spencer W. Kimball attests to this doctrine: "The *highest achievement of spirituality* comes as we conquer the flesh" (emphasis added).[48] President Harold B. Lee similarly taught, "Except [a man] learns to sacrifice of his appetites and desires in obedience to the laws of the gospel [he] cannot be sanctified and made holy before the Lord."[49]

Paradoxically, physical attainment is also a function of spiritual mastery, as Elder Hartman Rector, Jr. suggests:

> It is primarily the spirit that sees, hears, feels, knows passion and desire; it is the spirit that becomes addicted to drugs, bad habits, and evil desires. It is not just the physical body that is addicted, but the spirit also, which, of course, is the real you and me. We are spirits just as God is a spirit. Sometimes we make excuses for ourselves when we do what we should not do or

---

48 Spencer W. Kimball, "And the Lord Called His People Zion," *Ensign*, August 1984, 4.

49 Harold B. Lee, "For Every Child, His Spiritual and Cultural Heritage," *Children's Friend*, August 1943, 373.

fall short of what we should have done. We use such expressions as, "Oh! the spirit is willing but the flesh is weak." With such rationalizations we insinuate that it is completely our physical body's fault that we sin. In my opinion, this is not true. I believe the physical body is a very strong part of us and is of great benefit to us. Among other reasons, it was given to us to help us overcome our addictions, bad habits, and evil desires. The body is very obedient; generally speaking, it will do exactly what the spirit tells it to do. So it is not the physical body that we are struggling with; it is the spirit we must bring into subjection.[50]

The Dualistic Dimension of Discipleship

Personal conversion is an end in itself, but it is also a means to an end. In fact, ultimate conversion and sanctification will not occur unless we realize that fully coming to Christ is dependent on helping others come to Him as well. This dualistic dimension of discipleship was eloquently taught by Joseph Smith in his epistle relative to the work for the deceased wherein he declared: "Their salvation is necessary and essential to our salvation . . . they without us cannot be made perfect— neither can we without our dead be made perfect." (D&C 128. 15) The celestial kingdom will not be a place of spiritual seclusion where one finally escapes the mortal burden of caring for others. "Service is not something we endure on this earth so we can earn the right to live in the celestial kingdom," said President Marion G. Romney, "Service is the very fiber of which an exalted life in the celestial kingdom is made."[51]

---

50 Hartman, Rector, Jr., Conference Report, October 1970, 73.

51 Marion G. Romney, "The Celestial Nature of Self-reliance," *Ensign*, Nov. 1982, 93.

In essence, the twofold design of the gospel is to come unto Christ ourselves and to help others come unto Him. This includes extending help to Church members, nonmembers, and to those who have died without having the opportunity to receive the fullness of the gospel. To Peter, the Lord tenderly but firmly taught the principle thus: "I have prayed for thee that thy faith fail not: and when thou art converted, strengthen thy brethren." (Luke 22:32) Our salvation cannot come in any other way. The Psalmist declared: *"Create in me a clean heart, O God; and renew a right spirit within me.* Cast me not away from thy presence; and take not thy holy spirit from me. Restore unto me the joy of thy salvation; and uphold me with thy free spirit. *Then will I teach* transgressors thy ways; and sinners shall be converted unto thee" (Psalms 51:10-13; emphasis added; cf. D&C 11:21 and Joshua 1:11-15).

We have been commanded to share the gospel and to be a leaven to the world. We are to serve others and to teach them the verities of eternity. To teach spiritual things effectively we must first be spiritually effective ourselves. "Very little love can come from one who is not at peace with himself or herself and God," said Elder Marlin K. Jensen. "No one can be concerned about the welfare of someone else and give love to another until he or she has taken care of his or her own soul."[52] Only when we are converted, when we are grounded spiritually, can we help others do the same.

A Word of Caution

We cannot let our spiritual selves deteriorate and still maintain the ability to help others spiritually; we cannot help others gain and develop testimonies of the truth while not having done so ourselves. President Marion G. Romney taught that "spiritual guidance cannot come from the spiritually weak."[53] Paul warned: "Thou therefore which teachest another, teachest thou not

---

52. "A Union of Love and Understanding," *Ensign*, October 1994, 46–51.
53. *Ensign*, November 1982, 93.

thyself?" (Romans 2:21-22). To assume that we can seek the salvation of others while disregarding our own and that we will somehow receive an eternal reward for doing so is to err. The Book of Mormon chronicles the sad account of the seemingly helpful and promising Jaredite king Morianton, who nobly helped others but did not help himself: "And after that he had established himself king he did ease the burden of the people, by which he did gain favor in the eyes of the people, and they did anoint him to be their king. And *he did do justice unto the people, but not unto himself* because of his many whoredoms; wherefore *he was cut off from the presence of the Lord*" (Ether 10:10-11 emphasis added; cf. Omni 1:1-2).

The converse is also true. Whereas focusing on the salvation of others while disregarding our own won't do us much good, neither will focusing on *our* salvation while disregarding that of others. In fact, the two are so intricately interwoven that it is difficult to separate them. In other words, devotion to God, family, and others are complementary. Elder John A. Widtsoe declared this reality: "The Church is composed of homes. Church and home cannot be separated. Neither one come first. They are one."[54]

Proper Balance

Elder M. Russell Ballard counseled: "If you . . . search your hearts and courageously assess the priorities in your life, you may discover, as I did, that you need a better balance among your priorities."[55] We must always keep our priorities in perspective, so that we don't become unduly attentive to some while totally disregarding others. "As always there must be balance," said Elder Neal A. Maxwell, "the inordinate reading of the living scriptures that crowded out one's family, one's neighbors, and Christian service would be an error. One could become monastic though

---

54 John A. Widtsoe, *Evidences and Reconciliations*, 318.

55 M. Russell Ballard, Conference Report, Apr. 1987, 14–15; also *Ensign*, May 1987, 13

scholastic. Christian service to mankind could crowd out the living scriptures and become so consuming that one could forget his duties to family and to God, being a do-gooder almost as an escape from the family framework."[56]

While our absolute highest priority is the nurture of our personal relationship with God, this does not give us license to neglect (or abuse) spouse and children. Likewise, to nonchalantly say, "Well, my church callings are priority number four, so I guess I can skip home teaching this month" is not in the spirit of what the prophets have taught. So how do we do it? We cannot simply force into our lives everything and anything that will possibly fit. Elder Holland captured this principle beautifully with the following analogy:

> As a youth in England, Samuel Plimsoll was fascinated with watching ships load and unload their cargoes. He soon observed that, regardless of the cargo space available, each ship had its maximum capacity. If a ship exceeded its limit, it would likely sink at sea. In 1868 Plimsoll entered Parliament and passed a merchant shipping act that, among other things, called for making calculations of how much a ship could carry. As a result, lines were drawn on the hull of each ship in England. As the cargo was loaded, the freighter would sink lower and lower into the water. When the water level on the side of the ship reached the Plimsoll mark, the ship was considered loaded to capacity, regardless of how much space remained. As a result, British deaths at sea were greatly reduced. Like ships, people have differing capacities at different times and even different days in their lives. In our relationships we need to establish our own Plimsoll marks and

---

56 Neal A. Maxwell, *Things As They Really Are*, 106.

help identify them in the lives of those we love. Together we need to monitor the load levels and be helpful in shedding or at least readjusting some cargo if we see our sweetheart is sinking. Then, when the ship of love is stabilized, we can evaluate long-term what has to continue, what can be put off until another time, and what can be put off permanently. Friends, sweethearts, and spouses need to be able to monitor each other's stress and recognize the different tides and seasons of life. We owe it to each other to declare some limits and then help jettison some things if emotional health and the strength of loving relationships are at risk.[57]

Finding proper balance with our most important priorities is indeed challenging, especially when there are so many positive and worthwhile things to do. Even vigorous pursuit of what we consider worthwhile objectives can be fraught with danger. "Perpetual devotion to what a man calls his business is only to be sustained by perpetual neglect of many other things," said Robert Louis Stevenson, "and it is not by any means certain that a man's business is the most important thing he has to do."[58] Just because we are doing good things, we should not automatically assume we have our priorities straight. "Inordinate attention, even to good things, can diminish our devotion to God," counseled Elder Neal A. Maxwell,

For instance, one can be too caught up in sports and the forms of body worship we see among us. One can reverence nature and yet neglect nature's God. One can have an exclusionary regard for good music and similarly with a worthy profession.

57 Jeffrey R. Holland, "How Do I Love Thee?" *Brigham Young University 1999–2000 Speeches*, 158–62.

58 Robert Louis Stevenson, "An Apology for Idlers."

In such circumstances, the "weightier matters" are
often omitted (Matt. 23:23; see also 1 Cor. 2:16).
Only the Highest One can fully guide us as to the
highest good which you and I can do.[59]

Similarly Elder Richard G. Scott warned:

Are there so many fascinating, exciting things to
do or so many challenges pressing down upon
you that it is hard to keep focused on that which
is essential? When things of the world crowd
in, all too often the wrong things take highest
priority. Then it is easy to forget the fundamental
purpose of life. Satan has a powerful tool to use
against good people. It is distraction. He would
have good people fill life with "good things" so
there is no room for the essential ones. Have you
unconscientiously been caught in that trap?[60]

We may even innocently or naively mistake less important
issues and activities as being vital. C. S. Lewis portrayed the
dilemma thus:

There have been men before now who got so
interested in proving the existence of God that
they came to care nothing for God Himself
. . . as if the good Lord had nothing to do
but *exist!* There have been some who were so
occupied in spreading Christianity that they
never gave a thought to Christ. Man! Ye see it
in small matters. Did ye never know a lover of
books that with all his first editions and signed
copies had lost the power to read them? Or an
organiser of charities that had lost all love for
the poor? It is the subtlest of all the snares.[61]

59 Neal A. Maxwell, *Ensign*, May 2002, 37.
60 Richard G. Scott, Conference Report, April 2001, 6.
61 The Great Divorce, 73–74.

Illustratively, we can get so consumed with how we present the gospel that the message itself is blurred. Appearance and aesthetics, no matter how wonderful and appealing, must never be substituted nor be mistaken for substance and significance. Take, for example, the teacher who covers the table in the classroom with beautiful décor, yet fails to envelop her students with the beauty of true doctrine and spirit-filled testimony.

Conclusion

At times we can unconsciously or even knowingly insist on making our pursuit of spirituality a complex and arduous undertaking. To some the thought of putting God first may seem burdensome. Occasionally we hear the statement, "I never said it would be easy; I only said it would be worth it." However, the Savior never actually said this in scripture. In fact, there is a scriptural declaration to the contrary: "Take my yoke upon you . . , My yoke *is easy*, and my burden is light," said the Master. Alma reminded his son Helaman that it is "*easy* to give heed to the word of Christ, which will point to you a straight course to eternal bliss." Similarly, John extols that God's "commandments are not grievous" (Matthew 11.29-30; Alma 37:46; 1 John 5:3).

This is not to say that those who strive to live the gospel will be exempt from pain and sorrow. But it is nonetheless true that putting God first in our lives makes everything easier than it would be otherwise. Of this principle Elder A. Theodore Tuttle reminded us when he explained that the God's commandments "are for our good, and when we violate them, we suffer spiritually, physically, and emotionally. Remember . . . it's not nearly so hard to live the commandments as not to live them. The burden of keeping the commandments of the Lord is light compared to the burden of sin which we carry when we violate the commandments of God."[62]

President Ezra Taft Benson wisely counseled that "when we put God first, all other things fall into their proper place or drop

---

62 Theodore A. Tuttle, Conference Report, October 1965, 32.

out of our lives." [63] He also stated that "our love of the Lord will govern the claims for our affection, the demands on our time, the interests we pursue, and the order of our priorities."[64] What a promise! If we just put our first priority first, all other priorities in our life will fall into place as they should.

May we strive to do the will of the Lord and to feed ourselves spiritually so we may activate the power of the Atonement in our lives, and then, to the best of our ability, help our spouses, children, friends, and neighbors to do likewise. "The most important principle I can share," Elder Richard G. Scott declared, is to "anchor your life in Jesus Christ, your Redeemer. Make your Eternal Father and his Beloved Son the most important priority in your life—more important than life itself, more important than a beloved companion or children or anyone on earth. Make their will your central desire. Then all that you need for happiness will come to you.[65]

63 Ezra Taft Benson, *Ensign*, May 1988, 4.
64 Ibid.
65 Richard G. Scott, "The Power of Correct Principles," *Ensign*, May 1993, 34.

The Middoni Principle: Trusting God's Timing in Our Lives

"Scars have the strange power to remind us that our past is real."
—*Cormac McCarthy*, All the Pretty Horses

"It is a fearful thing to fall into the hands of the living God" (Hebrews 10:31). Paul's statement is true not only in the sense that God's vengeance brings fear upon the wicked, but putting our trust in God when we do not know the outcome can also be "a fearful thing." We may trust that God will deliver us, but we are often uncertain about the method of deliverance. Elder Harold B. Lee taught that obeying in faith even when we don't understand the reason is the difference between "blind" obedience and "intelligent" obedience.[66]

Adam offered "sacrifices unto the Lord" because he had been commanded to, even though he didn't know why the Lord had asked him to do it. It was only after his compliance that Adam learned: "This thing is a similitude of the sacrifice of the Only Begotten of the Father, which is full of grace and truth" (Moses 5:6–7). Adam was not guilty of blind obedience. Rather, there was an initial trust in his Heavenly Father based upon experience. He acted because he knew, as the Prophet Joseph Smith later

---

66 Harold B. Lee, *Improvement Era*, October 1962, 742.

taught, that "whatever God requires is right, no matter what it is, although we may not see the reason thereof until long after the events transpire."[67]

Not only should we always do what God requires, but we should also realize that, quite often, what we want or righteously desire is actually what the Lord wants; He just has a different way of orchestrating events than we sometimes initially contemplate. I call this the "Middoni Principle." Ammon and Lamoni demonstrated this kind of obedience—"intelligent" obedience— in their missionary labors in the land of Middoni

After much service and preaching among the people of King Lamoni, Ammon finally reaped the harvest of souls he had longed for. Among this harvest of converts was King Lamoni. After having tasted the precious "fruit" of the gospel, Lamoni experienced great joy and now desired now to share that joy (see 1 Nephi 8:12; Alma 36:24) with his family: "And it came to pass that when they had established a church in that land, that king Lamoni desired that Ammon should go with him to the land of Nephi, that he might show him unto his father" (Alma 20:1), who was the chief king in all the land (see Alma 20:8).

When Ammon asked the Lord if he should accompany Lamoni to see the chief king, his request was denied: "And the voice of the Lord came to Ammon, saying: Thou shalt not go up to the land of Nephi, for behold, the king [the chief king] will seek thy life; but thou shalt go to the land of Middoni; for behold, thy brother Aaron, and also Muloki and Ammah are in prison" (Alma 20:2). When Lamoni learned of this revelation, he gave his wholehearted support and even volunteered his personal services to free Ammon's brethren.

At this point the story takes a strange turn. While journeying to Middoni, Ammon and Lamoni encountered the chief king, who, upon seeing the Nephite with his son, sought to take Ammon's life. His attempt, however, was unsuccessful. Why

---

67 Joseph Smith, *Teachings of the Prophet Joseph Smith*, comp. Joseph Fielding Smith (Salt Lake City: Deseret Book, 1976), 256.

would the Lord tell Ammon to go to Middoni and not visit Lamoni's father in Nephi if they end up encountering him anyhow? The Lord knew that Ammon and Lamoni would meet the chief king. Perhaps the issue with the Lord was not "What is the best way to protect Ammon?" but rather "What is the best way to bring about the conversion of the chief king?" God does intervene to save and protect, but He can never force the conversion of a soul (see Helaman 14:30–31; 2 Nephi 10:23–24; see also "Know This, That Every Soul Is Free," *Hymns*, no. 240).

God does, however, take a hand in shaping the circumstances and events surrounding the conversion of the soul. Perhaps being away from the security of home was precisely what King Lamoni's father needed in order for a change of heart. Perhaps the initial trek toward Middoni and the subsequent meeting in the wilderness was a more effective way for God to show the chief king "the great love [that Ammon] had for his son Lamoni" (Alma 20:26). Furthermore, once Ammon withstood the king and the king had to listen, he "was greatly astonished at the words which [Ammon] had spoken, and also at the words which had been spoken by his son Lamoni, therefore he was desirous to learn them" (Alma 20:27). Sometimes the only way the Lord can get our attention is when He takes us out of our comfort zones.

King Lamoni's desire to share the gospel with his father was a righteous desire that was fulfilled in a peculiar manner. We all have moments in life when we want spiritually to "go up to the land of Nephi," as it were, for whatever righteous reason. The real test comes when the Lord tells us to "go to the land of Middoni" instead. When this happens it is imperative that we not only do what the Lord says, but that we realize that in so doing it is likely that our original desired outcome just might be fulfilled, albeit in a better way. Scriptures, ancient and modern, speak to the truth of this principle. Proverbs 14:12 states, "There is a way which seemeth right unto a man, but the end thereof are the ways of death." The same idea is found in Isaiah: "For my thoughts are

not your thoughts, neither are your ways my ways, saith the Lord"
(Isaiah 55:8). And President Wilford Woodruff said, "We should
begin to understand that God's ways are infinitely superior to
our ways, and that His counsels, though they may seem to call
for sacrifice, are always the best and the safest for us to adopt
and carry out."[68] What we desire in righteousness is often what
the Lord desires, although His method in fulfilling our desire is
often different from what we would expect.

When tensions ran high in Missouri in 1834, various Saints
in Kirtland and surrounding areas joined in the march of Zion's
Camp in order to give relief to the suffering Saints in Zion and
to help restore their property. The command of the Lord fueled
their cause: "Behold, I say unto you, the redemption of Zion
must needs come by power" (D&C 103:15). In the aftermath
of several months of arduous and painful events, some would
conclude that Zion's Camp was unsuccessful. The distressed
Saints in Zion were relieved to some extent, but their lands
were not recovered. Was Zion's Camp a failure? To those who
understand the "Middoni principle" it was not. As President
Wilford Woodruff later explained:

> We gained an experience that we never could
> have gained in any other way. We had the
> privilege of beholding the face of the prophet,
> and we had the privilege of travelling a thousand
> miles with him, and seeing the workings of the
> Spirit of God with him, and the revelations of
> Jesus Christ unto him and the fulfilment of
> those revelations. And he gathered some two
> hundred Elders from throughout the nation in
> that early day and sent us broadcast into the
> world to preach the Gospel of Jesus Christ.
> Had I not gone up with Zion's Camp I should

68 James R. Clark, ed., *Messages of the First Presidency*, 6 vols. (Salt Lake
City: Bookcraft, 1965–75), 3:145.

not have been here to-day, and I presume that
would have been the case with many others. . . .
By going there we were thrust into the vineyard
to preach the Gospel, and the Lord accepted
our labors.[69]

Elder Orson F. Whitney understood this principle as well.
Concerning the redemption of Zion by power, he stated: "The
redemption of Zion is more than the purchase or recovery of
lands, the building of cities, or even the founding of nations.
It is the conquest of the heart, the subjugation of the soul,
the sanctifying of the flesh, the purifying and ennobling of the
passions."[70] Interestingly, a revelation regarding the land in
Zion states: "In time ye shall possess the goodly land" (D&C
103:20). It is apparent that the Lord's plan for the redemption
of Zion was different than what was expected by some of the
Saints.

Similarly, many Jews at the time of Christ failed to recognize
the promised Messiah, not because of lack of expectation but due
to their incorrect understanding of what type of Messiah would
come. The Jews expected a political leader to free them from
Roman oppression, not a suffering servant to free them from
sin (see Isaiah 53). When we lean on our own understanding
and forget to trust in the Lord, we are inherently insisting that
our wisdom is above the Lord's. Elder Neal A. Maxwell wrote:
"When we are unduly impatient with circumstances, we may be
suggesting that we know what is best—better than does God.
Or, at least, we are asserting that our timetable is better than His.
Either way, we are questioning the reality of God's omniscience
as if, as some seem to believe, God were on some sort of post-
doctoral fellowship, trying to complete His understanding

---

69 *Journal of Discourses*, 26 vols. (Liverpool: F. D. Richards & Sons, 1851–
     86), 13:158.

70 *The Life of Heber C. Kimball* (Salt Lake City: Bookcraft, 1973), 65.

and, therefore, needing to use us as consultants."[71] On another occasion Elder Maxwell wrote: "We do not control what I call the great transfer board in the sky. The inconveniences that are sometimes associated with release from our labors here are necessary in order to accelerate the work there. Heavenly Father can't do His work with ten times more people than we have on this planet, except He will on occasion take some of the very best sisters and brothers. The conditions of termination here, painful though they are, are a part of the conditions of acceleration there. Thus we are back to *faith in the timing of God, and to be able to say Thy timing be done*, even when we do not fully understand it" (CES Fireside, 2 Feb. 2001).

The Middoni principle entails more than mere obedience. "Obedience [is not] a mindless shifting of our personal responsibility," Elder Maxwell declared. "Instead, it is tying ourselves to a living God who will introduce us—as soon as we are ready—to new and heavier responsibilities involving situations of high adventure. Obedience, therefore, is not evasion; it is an invasion—one that takes us deep into the realm of our possibilities."[72] Intelligent obedience coupled with the knowledge that God's ways are higher than ours allows us to trust that all things will work for our benefit in the long run.

God's Timing and Trials

One way we accept God's timing in our lives is by trying to understand the purpose of trials and suffering and why bad things sometimes happen to good people. In my work at various secondary schools and university campuses over the past twenty-two years, I have been intrigued, if not mystified, by the relative ease with which some students are willing to buy into a new paradigm on the basis of just about any pretext: convenience,

---

71 Neal A. Maxwell, *Notwithstanding My Weakness* (Salt Lake City: Deseret Book, 1981), 59–60.

72 Neal A. Maxwell, *All These Things Shall Give Thee Experience* (Salt Lake City: Deseret Book, 1980), 127.

peer pressure, popularity, political correctness, etc. Many of these quickly accepted notions are not thought out to their logical conclusions, thus leaving some students with philosophic jars of "snake-oil" to be set out as décor on their intellectual coffee tables.

One such philosophy that seems to crop up over and over again is a popular atheistic sound-bite which seemingly disproves, in an instant as it were, the existence of God or any sort of divine being. Usually this notion is couched in various forms of "if-then" statements, punctuated with stern facial expressions of certitude and conviction. The catchphrase goes like this: "If there really is a God, He would not allow so much suffering and violence on this earth!" In philosophic circles the conundrum is often termed "the logical problem of evil." Such an argument is age old. Illustratively, Epicurus, famed philosopher of old, postulated: "Either God is unwilling to prevent evil or He is unable. If He is unwilling, then He cannot be perfectly good; if He is unable, then He cannot be all powerful."[73]

Here we have the perfect example of too quickly making assumptions when one does not yet have the big picture, of not seeing the forest for the trees. Such a position seems reasonable at first glance, but think of the logic it betrays. The assumption is that if there really were a God, He would certainly be a "good" God ("Good" meaning whatever brings pleasure or joy to man from his perspective) and therefore only capable of producing and embracing "good" things. Since there is plenty of "bad" in the world, there must certainly not be a God. It is intriguing, if not ironic, that this atheistic argument is often couched in a rigid definition of who and what God is. (As if an atheist, who by definition does not believe in the existence of God, knew for certain what God can and cannot be!) But surely this is an odd reason not to accept the existence of God. To pin one's beliefs on such inane logic is untenable. To make such a statement reminds me of what Grant Bangerter once said: "Two Russians

73 David L. Paulson, BYU Forum address, Sept. 21, 1999.

went around the world in a spacecraft a time or two and declared that they had gone to heaven and God was not there. This is a pretty weak argument for atheism. It isn't even scientific."[74]

While studying at Purdue University, I took an advanced graduate class in the sociology of religion. In one of his first lectures, my professor revealed his orientation on these matters: "A person who is religious might say something like this, 'Man was created in God's image' but a religious sociologist says 'No, God is created in man's image.'"

Once again, while such axioms seem plausible and appealing at first glance, they lack substance when one tries to ground them in logic and proof. Elder Neal A. Maxwell put the dilemma this way:

> Man is too provincial to fashion any new morality which is true morality. For just as atheism is too simple, man's mortality will always bear the stamp of his environment and the imprint of his particular problems; the response cannot be whole, because man is not whole in his perspective, in his experience, or in his love. He may make facsimiles, using the real morality as a model, but the flaws in his counterfeits are fatal and detectable for anyone who cares about the real thing.[75]

The Book of Mormon addresses these popular, atheistic notions in plausible, logical, and practical ways. Alma not only addressed "the logical problem of evil," he also provided a thoughtful and well-grounded argument against the atheistic position. After being imprisoned and abused, Alma and Amulek were compelled to witness the destruction by fire of the scriptures and of those who believed in God. Amulek protested, insisting that they stretch forth their hands to save those engulfed in the

74 *Ensign*, Nov.1979, 9.
75 Neal A. Maxwell, "For the Power Is in Them . . ." *Mormon Musings*, 52.

flames: "And when Amulek saw the pains of the women and children who were consuming in the fire, he also was pained; and he said unto Alma: How can we witness this awful scene? Therefore let us stretch forth our hands, and exercise the power of God which is in us, and save them from the flames." In response, Alma said, "The Spirit constraineth me that I must not stretch forth mine hand; for behold the Lord receiveth them up unto himself, in glory; and he doth suffer that they may do this thing, or that the people may do this thing unto them, according to the hardness of their hearts, that the judgments which he shall exercise upon them in his wrath may be just; and the blood of the innocent shall stand as a witness against them, yea, and cry mightily against them at the last day."

Implied in Alma's words is the fact that sometimes awful things happen to good people. God must let all people (for good or bad) make their choices. Alma understood that God allows the wicked not only to choose evil in their hearts but to act out that evil. For the punishment to be just, the act must be realized. God cannot punish the wicked for evil acts that are stopped by Him in the first place or else man would have no agency.

President Spencer W. Kimball makes this unmistakably clear:

> Now, we find many people critical when a righteous person is killed, a young father or mother is taken from a family, or when violent deaths occur. Some become bitter when oft-repeated prayers seem unanswered. Some lose faith and turn sour when solemn administrations . . . seem to be ignored and no restoration seems to come from repeated prayer. . . . But if all the sick were healed, if all the righteous were protected and the wicked destroyed, the whole program of the Father would be annulled and the basic principle of

the Gospel, free agency, would be ended. If pain and sorrow and total punishment immediately followed the doing of evil, no soul would repeat a misdeed. If joy and peace and rewards were instantaneously given the doer of good, there could be no evil—all would do good and not because of the rightness of doing good. There would be no test of strength, no development of character, no growth of powers, no free agency ... Should all prayers be immediately answered according to our selfish desires and our limited understanding, then there would be little or no suffering, sorrow, disappointment, or even death; and if these were not, there would also be an absence of joy, success, resurrection, eternal life, and godhood."[76]

The Divine Purpose of Trials

How important it is to trust in God's timing and His allowance of trials in our lives. Various reasons can be cited as to why trials are for our benefit. For one, trials bring needed experience. Orson F. Whitney declared: "No pain that we suffer, no trial that we experience is wasted. It ministers to our education, to the development of such qualities as patience, faith, fortitude and humility. All that we suffer and all that we endure, especially when we endure it patiently, builds up our characters, purifies our hearts, expands our souls, and makes us more tender and charitable, more worthy to be called the children of God, and it is through sorrow and suffering, toil and tribulation, that we gain the education that we come here to acquire." (In *Improvement Era*, Mar. 1966, 211) When accept this fact, we are able to spend more time learning from our trials and less time complaining to the heavens about them. "When we are unduly impatient

---

76 Spencer W. Kimball, *Improvement Era*, March 1966, 180, 210.

with circumstances," said Elder Neal A. Maxwell, "we may be suggesting that we know what is best-better than does God. Or, at least, we are asserting that our timetable is better than His. Either way, we are questioning the reality of God's omniscience as if, as some seem to believe, God were on some sort of post-doctoral fellowship, trying to complete His understanding and, therefore, needing to use us as consultants."

Additionally, wise are those individuals who realize that trials and blessings go hand in hand. Elder Maxwell perceptively observed: "So often in life a deserved blessing is quickly followed by a needed stretching. Spiritual exhilaration may be quickly followed by a vexation or temptation. Were it otherwise, extended spiritual reveries or immunities from adversity might induce in us a regrettable forgetfulness of others in deep need. The sharp, side-by-side contrast of the sweet and the bitter is essential until the very end of this brief, mortal experience." Trials, then, are our constant companions, albeit not always desired ones. Furthermore, trials are tailor-made for each person. President Howard W. Hunter's instruction is poignant: "Obviously, the personal burdens of life vary from person to person, but every one of us has them. Furthermore, each trial in life is tailored to the individual's capacities and needs as known by a loving Father in Heaven."[77] Similarly, Elder Bruce R. McConkie taught: "Our Eternal Father knows all of his spirit children, and in his infinite wisdom, he chooses the very time that each comes to earth to gain a mortal body and undergo a probationary experience. Everything the Lord does is for the benefit and blessing of his children. And each of those children is subjected to the very trials and experiences that Omniscient Wisdom knows he should have."[78]

A seemingly paradoxical aspect of trials is that though they often come packaged as tragedies and disappointments, they also come in the form of prosperity, blessings, and success. With

77 Howard W. Hunter, *Ensign*, Nov. 1990, 18.
78 Bruce R. McConkie, *Millennial Messiah*, 660.

either, it's wise to turn heavenward in both good times and our bad. "Turning to the Savior can also protect us against our successes," said Virginia Pearce. "We see everyday evidence of how success can result in destroying a person's soul. The media holds up lives ruined by success. What if, on a daffodil day, we really, really think that all of the good things in our lives are there because we are simply so smart, so talented, so effective in everything we enjoy comes as a direct result of our work and brains? Do you see my point? Pride and egotism injure a soul as surely as do the bitterness and pain of affliction and failure. Success is an affliction to the soul unless it is recognized for what it is—God's working in our lives. With success, as well as adversity, we pray that our performance will be consecrated for the welfare of our souls. And he will do that, because each prayer we offer will somehow be an expression that we are joyfully, voluntarily, and quietly desiring to give our lives to him. Then desperate days refine us rather then destroy us. And daffodil days become days of worship and gratitude rather than days of pride and boasting." Similarly, Elder Boyd K. Packer gave this profound advice: "The crucial test of life, I repeat, does not center in the choice between fame and obscurity, nor between wealth and poverty. The greatest decision of life is between good and evil. We may foolishly bring unhappiness and trouble, even suffering upon ourselves. These are not always to be regarded as penalties imposed by a displeased Creator. They are part of the lessons of life, part of the test. Some are tested by poor health, some by a body that is deformed or homely. Others are tested by handsome and healthy bodies; some by the passion of youth; others by the erosions of age. Some suffer disappointment in marriage, family problems; others live in poverty and obscurity. Some (perhaps this is the hardest test) find ease and luxury. All are part of the test, and there is more equality in this testing than sometimes we suspect."[79]

---

79 Boyd K. Packer, "The Choice," *Ensign*, Nov. 1980, 21.

We would do well to trust that God knows best and that all things will give us experience and will be for our ultimate good (see D&C 122:7). We show this trust by doing His will and recognizing His guiding hand in all things. As we do this we will begin to feel and understand God's infinite love and concern for us and for our loved ones struggling through disappointment, grief, and sorrow. Ultimately we begin to realize that trials are definitely not evidence that God does not love us or that he simply doesn't care. Elder Maxwell stated that "God [is not] a kindly grandfather who would indulge mankind in whatever they wish to do. . . . Our is a loving Father who will, if necessary, let come to each of us some harsh life experiences, that we might learn that his love for us is so great and so profound that he will let us suffer, as he did his Only Begotten Son In the flesh, that his and our triumph and learning might be complete and full."[80]

---

80 Neal A. Maxwell, in "Charge to Religious Educators," 97.

Wasted Time, Lost Opportunities, and Good Intentions

OVER THE YEARS, I'VE BEEN amazed at the incredible competence and consecration demonstrated by Church members, seminary and institute employees, and volunteer teachers as they fulfill their callings and assignments. Surely one of the signs of the true Church in the last days is the unmatched selflessness and commitment of Latter-day Saints in building God's kingdom here on earth. How perplexing it is, then, to discover that we are actually often "living below [our] privileges."[81] With so little time, why don't we make the most of every minute, every opportunity? Fortunately, there are doctrines that can help us refocus and recharge when we realize we've wasted time or lost opportunities.

The Gospel of Grace and Good Intentions

Wise are those who learn to be "doers of the word, and not hearers only" (James 1:22). To this end, Elder Holland's words are instructive:

> Above all else we can live the gospel. Surely there is no more powerful missionary message we can send to this world than the example of a loving and happy Latter-day Saint life. The

---

81 Dieter F. Uchtdorf, *Ensign*, April 2011.

manner and bearing, the smile and kindness
of a faithful member of the Church brings a
warmth and an outreach which no missionary
tract or videotape can convey. People do not
join the Church because of what they know.
They join because of what they feel, what they
see and want spiritually. Our spirit of testimony
and happiness in that regard will come through
to others if we let it. *Asking every member to be a
missionary is not nearly as crucial as asking every
member to be a member!*"[82]

It is purported that St. Francis of Assisi once admonished,
"Always preach the gospel, and when necessary, use words!"[83]
People often learn more from our actions than from what we say.

So what about good desires or intentions? It's been said
that "the road to hell is paved with good intentions." This
catchphrase is indeed catchy. But is it true? In speaking of the
gifts of the spirit the Lord informs us that "they are given for
the benefit of *those who love me and keep all my commandments*,
and him *that seeketh so to do*" (D&C 46:9; emphasis added).
While it's important to keep the commandments, how many
of us truly keep *all* of God's commandments? Just One. How
fortunate, how merciful, how compassionate it is that God also
rewards those that *seek* to do good. How fortunate indeed that
a willing heart makes a difference to the Lord: "Behold, the
Lord requireth the heart and a willing mind; and *the willing*
and obedient shall eat the good of the land of Zion in these last
days" (D&C 64:34). We may be tempted to lump the willing
and the obedient together, but in the gospel of Jesus Christ,
desires alone are divinely considered and clearly count. Elder
Oaks wisely counseled:

---

82 Jeffery R. Holland, Conference Report, April 2001.
83 As found in Richard H. Cracroft, "Preach the Gospel . . . and if Necessary . . . " BYU Magazine Fall 2002.

When someone wanted to do something for my father-in-law but was prevented by circumstances, he would say, 'Thank you. I will take the good will for the deed.' Similarly, I believe that our Father in Heaven will receive the true desires of our hearts as a substitute for actions that are genuinely impossible. Here we see another contrast between the laws of God and the laws of men. It is entirely impractical to grant a legal advantage on the basis of an intent not translated into action. 'I intended to sign that contract,' or 'We intended to get married,' cannot stand as the equivalent of the act required by law. If the law were to give effect to intentions in lieu of specific acts, it would open the door for too much abuse, since the laws of man have no reliable means of determining our inner-most thoughts. In contrast, the law of God can reward a righteous desire because an omniscient God can discern it. As revealed through the prophet of this dispensation, God 'is a discerner of the thoughts and intents of the heart.' (D&C 33:1.) If a person refrains from a particular act because he is genuinely unable to perform it, but truly would if he could, our Heavenly Father will know this and will reward that person accordingly."[84]

The Savior taught in the Sermon on the Mount a higher standard that holds men accountable not only for their actions but for the desires of their hearts as well. If we are accountable for the evil thoughts and desires we have, then surely the same holds true for righteous thoughts as well. No wonder we are reminded to "watch [ourselves], and *[our] thoughts*, and *[our] words*, and [our] deeds" (Mosiah 4:30).

---

84 *Ensign*, June 1986, 66.

When might an individual be rewarded for righteous desires not put into action? Perhaps an individual with dietary restrictions is prohibited from fasting. Consider the man who desires to donate to a charitable foundation but who, with razor-thin finances and must, of necessity, abstain from giving. King Benjamin offered this insight: "And again, I say unto the poor, ye who have not and yet have sufficient, that ye remain from day to day; I mean all you who deny the beggar, because ye have not; I would that ye say in your hearts that: I give not because I have not, but if I had I would give. And now, if ye say this in your hearts ye remain guiltless" (Mosiah 4:24–25). President Lorenzo Snow spoke comfort when he said,

> There is no Latter-day Saint who dies after having lived a faithful life who will lose anything because of having failed to do certain things when opportunities were not furnished him or her. In other words, if a young man or a young woman has no opportunity of getting married, and they live faithful lives up to the time of their death, they will have all the blessings, exaltation, and glory that any man or woman will have who had this opportunity and improved it. That is sure and positive."[85]

Similarly, President Boyd K. Packer once said:

> Those who do not marry or those who cannot have children are not excluded from the eternal blessings they seek but which, for now, remain beyond their reach. We do not always know how or when blessings will present themselves, but the promise of eternal increase will not be denied any faithful individual who makes and

---

85 *The Teachings of Lorenzo Snow*, comp. Clyde J. Williams, Salt Lake City: Bookcraft, 1984, 138; see also President Howard W. Hunter, CR, October 1994.

keeps sacred covenants. Your secret yearnings and tearful pleadings will touch the heart of both the Father and the Son. You will be given a personal assurance from Them that your life will be full and that no blessing that is essential will be lost to you. As a servant of the Lord, acting in the office to which I have been ordained, I give those in such circumstances a promise that there will be nothing essential to your salvation and exaltation that shall not in due time rest upon you. Arms now empty will be filled, and hearts now hurting from broken dreams and yearning will be healed.[86]

We must take care not to judge unrighteously, give others the benefit of the doubt in difficult circumstances, counsel in love and charity, trust in scriptural principles, and be sensitive to situations that require discernment, patience, and understanding. This is especially important for Church leaders. True it is that a Church leader "does not represent the people to the prophet but the prophet to the people" and should thus never "forget which way [they] face!"[87] However, this does not mean that a Church leader categorically ignores the needs of members nor callously responds with blatant indifference when those he serves have legitimate concerns or questions.

The Gospel of Repentance and Lost Opportunities

LDS Church leaders and religious educators often encourage their classes and congregations with this oft-quoted statement: "It is better to prepare and prevent, rather than repair and repent."[88] While inherently true, such statements need not

86 Pres. Packer, "The Witness," April 2014.

87 President Packer as quoted by Elder Lynn G. Robbins, October General Conference 2014.

88 Although not the originator of this statement, President Ezra Taft Benson often used this axiom. For example, see "The Law of Chastity," Brigham Young University Devotional, Provo, Utah, Oct. 13, 1987.

imply that repentance is thus a flawed "plan B" approach to our mortal probation. Accordingly, those in need of mercy and forgiveness must not conclude that they will be forever flawed and left wanting, even after repenting. On the other hand, an individual in sin must not react bitterly to this principle. By so doing they may deprive themselves of much-needed humility that should be realized as a consequence of their transgressions. Indeed, it is this very humility and associated godly sorrow that becomes the catalyst and facilitating agent for true and lasting repentance. Unfortunately, those who demand mercy sometimes ignore or downplay the importance of justice. Likewise, some who become overzealous with justice may be prone to diminish the validity and need for mercy. Finding balance between these two principles is challenging yet needful.

There is a wonderful principle found in sections 66 and 75 of the Doctrine and Covenants, which, if understood and properly applied, can give added understanding to the process of repentance and the corresponding miracle of forgiveness of sin. This principle likewise helps discerning souls to properly balance the principles of justice and mercy while understanding the sobering truth that true repentance does not mitigate certain lost opportunities in life that come as a result of sin.

Background on Sections 66 and 75

Section 66 came as a response to a request made by William E. McLellin to know the Lord's will concerning him. At the time this revelation was given, McLellin was in relatively good standing with the Church. He was born January 18, 1806, in Smith County, Tennessee. He joined the Church at age twenty-five and a few years later, in 1835, was called as one of the original members of the Quorum of the Twelve Apostles. McLellin, a schoolteacher by profession, had many instances where he demonstrated dedicated service to the Church, yet his problematic relationship with Church leaders and doctrines eventually lead to his excommunication in 1838. He is generally remembered as the individual who failed miserably in his attempt to produce or write a supposed revelation from God. This attempt came in response to the criticism of certain Church members and their disdain for the wording of the revelations extant in the soon-to-be published Doctrine and Covenants. The Lord in essence issued a challenge (see D&C 67:6–7) to see if the "most wise" among the members of the Church could create a revelation comparable to "even the least" of the existing revelations. If it were possible to create such a revelation, it would justify some of the Church member's position that the revelations were not of God. Deemed the most intelligent member at the time, McLellin was chosen, but he ultimately failed.[89]

In section 66 the Lord commends McLellin for turning away from iniquity and accepting the truth of the fullness of the gospel (see vv. 1–2). The Lord warns him, however, that he is not completely free from sin and specifically warns him of weaknesses with respect to tendencies and temptations to violate the law of chastity (see v. 10). The Lord extends the invitation to McLellin to serve a mission in the "eastern lands" (v. 7) and gives him guidance and instruction relative to this mission. These items of instruction, the mission call, the warnings, and other items of counsel, were given on October 25, 1831. Although McLellin and his companion, Samuel Smith, did commence this mission on November 16, 1831, they were not able to continue for long. Explaining the reason for limited service, Samuel Smith stated, "We went a short distance, but because of disobedience, our way was hedged up before us."[90]

Several months later, on January 25, 1832, another revelation was received which, in part, again revealed the Lord's will relative to William E. McLellin and his call to serve a mission. In this

---

89 See *History of the Church,* 1:226.
90 As found in Shipp and Welch, *The Journals of William E. McLellin,* 300. Original quote in Samuel H. Smith Journal, 1831–33, LDS Church Archives.

revelation (section 75) the Lord chastens him for his sins and murmurings (see vv. 7–8) and emphatically declares: "I revoke the commission which I gave unto him to go unto the eastern countries" (v. 6). The Lord then says, "I forgive him and say unto him again, Go ye into the south countries" (v. 8).[91] Joseph Fielding Smith explained: "William E. McLellin was rebuked for his failure to magnify a commission which had been given him, and this commission was revoked. He was now appointed to travel with diligence and to labor with his might, as were all the others, but *he was to go to the south while formerly he was sent to the east.* The Lord, once more forgave him for his disobedience and he was to have as a companion Luke Johnson."[92]

Despite the fact that McLellin eventually apostatized from the Church, this canonized revelation in the Doctrine and Covenants still has relevant application for each one of us. The purpose in presenting the following is not to hold McLellin up as any sort of positive example but rather to "liken the scriptures" to ourselves by showing not only what the Lord was willing to do for William McLellin, but more importantly, what He is willing and able to do for us.

Understanding the Principle

Boyd K. Packer observed, "A principle is an enduring truth, a law, a rule you can adopt to guide you in making decisions. *Generally principles are not spelled out in detail.* That leaves you

---

91 In Hoyt Brewster's *D&C Encyclopedia* (pp. 547–48) "south countries" (D&C 75:6–8) is explained as follows: "This charge did not include territory foreign to the United States, but merely meant he was to go into the southern states, or, that country which was south of his present location. Similarly, Major Ashley and Burr Riggs were sent into the 'south country' (D&C 75:17)."

92 *Church History and Modern Revelation* (Salt Lake City, Utah: The Council of The Twelve Apostles, 1946), p. 46; emphasis added. A similar situation occurs in the Book of Mormon with Alma's wayward son Corianton. He is rebuffed for immorality (see Alma 39) but is ultimately called again to preach the gospel (see Alma 42:31).

free to find your way with an enduring truth, a principle, as your anchor."[93] In light of Elder Packer's definition, it is interesting to note that neither the Doctrine and Covenants nor Samuel Smith specifically reveal what William E. McLellin's shortcoming was, only that he sinned and was forgiven. The fact that things were not "spelled out" in more detail invites us to discover a scriptural principle we can apply to our lives.

McLellin sinned but was then forgiven and subsequently given another chance to serve a mission. However, the call to go to the eastern lands was revoked. The principle here, simply stated, is this: although the Lord is willing and able to forgive, that does not preclude us from suffering certain consequences. In this case, an opportunity was forever lost—the opportunity Elder McLellin had of fulfilling a mission call to the East. Although a similar opportunity was presented later, along with the promised forgiveness, the fact of the matter is that this particular opportunity was lost forever. With that lost opportunity, one can only speculate about all of the experiences, associations, spiritual growth, and overall good that could have been realized had McLellin fulfilled his call to the East. Forgiveness is real, and our Father in Heaven is willing and able to forgive when we follow His plan. But forgiveness does not bring about an automatic reinstatement of all opportunities and blessings we may have squandered. Sin can cause individuals to miss out on certain opportunities in life—opportunities that, as is often the case, are lost in this lifetime.

The repentant transgressor can go on in faithful service in the kingdom, yet despite the miracle of forgiveness, sin can leave and indelible mark on our *mortal* lives. This principle is vividly portrayed in the following story from the life of President Spencer W. Kimball:

---

93 "The Word of Wisdom: The Principle and the Promises," *Ensign,* May 1996, 17.

One day, I came home from school to find one of the horses tangled in the wire fence, bleeding profusely. He had been struggling to extricate himself and had cut deep gashes in his shoulder and legs. I shall never forget that day. As I remember it, the larger gash was about six inches long and so deep that a heavy piece of flesh and hide hung down, leaving an ugly bleeding wound. What could I do? There was no veterinary in the town, my father was away, the neighbor men were at work, and perhaps none of the boys in the area could do any better than I could do and time was of the essence, and so I faced the task, with the help of my sister, realizing that at best, I might do a clumsy job, but there was no alternative. I must try. I washed the wound with hot soapy water, spread over the gash some of the common liniment we always had for our animals, and, with a large needle and common thread, I began to sew it together. When I pushed the needle through his sensitive flesh and skin, he jumped back and struck at me with his front feet and bit me on the arm. I had some mixed emotions at this juncture as I nursed my own wound. Here I was trying so hard to relieve him and this was the thanks I received. I realized he did not fully comprehend what I was trying so earnestly to do for him. Now, I put a noose on his lower lip with a stick in it and twisted his lip so that his attention was turned to his lip agony while I could sew up the gash and get the wound fixed so it could heal itself. I had my little sister hold the noose tight. In and out, I pushed the needle

through the quivering flesh until the edges of
the wound were tied tight together. Even after
I had released the noose and the wound was
firmly sewed together, I was still sure that this
horse never knew nor fully realized what I had
done for him. If he remembered me at all, it
was probably as the one who had pricked his
tender flesh with needles and severely pinched
his lip in a noose. *The wound healed. There was
always an ugly scar on the shoulder but the horse
lived to give much service on the little farm.*[94]

Often, there are visible and invisible scars left upon the
repentant sinner that cannot be removed during one's mortal
lifetime. An example of this is an individual who becomes a
chronic smoker, later changes his ways, and subsequently endures
the rest of his life in faithful abstinence—but with irreparable
lung damage. Even though he may repent, there are things he can
never get back. The same with a latter-day youth who is involved
in illicit sexual relations resulting in such things as pregnancy,
defilement, emotional damage, and sexual disease—all these
may leave permanent scars. Yes, such a youth may repent, have a
change of heart, and endure faithfully in the covenant; but that
does not mitigate the fact that there are certain consequences
they must live with for the rest of their mortal lives.

An example of this can be seen in Elder Ballard's warning
to prospective missionaries: "Please understand this: the bar
that is the standard for missionary service is being raised. The
day of the 'repent and go' missionary is over. You know what
I'm talking about, don't you, my young brothers? Some young
men have the mistaken idea that they can be involved in sinful
behavior and then repent when they're 18 1/2 so they can go

---

94 *The Teachings of Spencer W. Kimball,* edited by Edward L. Kimball (Salt
   Lake City: Bookcraft, 1982), 91–92.

on their mission at 19. *While it is true that you can repent of sins, you may or you may not qualify to serve.*"⁹⁵ Such a concept may seem harsh to some, but it underscores the seriousness of sin and wasted opportunities in the never-to-be-repeated days of one's youth. Joseph F. Smith lamented this awful predicament:

> I wish that all young men could appreciate the value there is in this practice and in giving their youthful days to the service of the Lord. Growth, development, progress, self-respect, the esteem and admiration of men naturally follow such a course in youth. . . . Waiting to serve the Lord until the wild oats of youth are sown, is reprehensible. There is always something lacking the man who spends his youth in wickedness and sin, and then turns to righteousness in later years. Of course, the Lord honors his repentance, and it is better far that a man should late turn from evil than to continue in sin all his days, but the fact is clear that the best part of his life and strength is wasted. . . . There are regrets and heartburnings in repenting late in life from the follies and sins of youth, but there are consolation and rich reward in serving the Lord in the vigorous days of early manhood.⁹⁶

God is merciful to the repentant sinner. Forgiveness is real. Sin, however, can carry consequences long after an individual has completely repented. The Book of Mormon speaks of the sons of Mosiah in this regard: "For they were the very vilest of sinners. And the Lord saw fit in his infinite mercy to spare them; *nevertheless they suffered much anguish of soul because of their iniquities*" (Mosiah 28:4; emphasis added). Even after mighty

95 In Conference Report, Oct. 2002; italics added.
96 *Gospel Doctrine* (Salt Lake City: Deseret Book, 1939), 334–35.

change of heart, they still had to repair much of the damage they'd done (see Mosiah 27:34–35). Perhaps there were things they were never able to completely repair—wounded hearts, their own reputations, etc. How sobering to realize that the availability of God's forgiveness cannot change or turn back the unrelenting forward motion of the clock of opportunity.

The second crucial principle relative to President Kimball's story is that although sin is serious—indeed, very serious—there really is repentance. There really is forgiveness and healing. There really can be a genuine change of heart and a return to purity. The horse in the story went on to give "much service on the little farm." The fact that one may have missed opportunities or lifelong trials caused by sin does not mean they are disqualified from eternal life. Did they miss out on certain blessings and joy in this earth life? Yes. Are they ultimately cast out from God's presence? No. Not as long as there is sincere and lasting repentance.

Care must be taken by teachers and leaders not to steal hope from starving souls who sincerely come back to the table of the Lord only to be mistakenly left to think that dinner scraps are all that remain. Individuals who sincerely repent must not rob themselves of this divine hope either. It is a precarious thing to deny others (ourselves included) of the Lord's mercy. In the Book of Mormon we read of the prophet Zenock, who taught, "Thou art *angry*, O Lord, with this people, because *they will not understand thy mercies which thou hast bestowed upon them because of thy Son*" (Alma 33:16). To fret, complain, or murmur about the availability of grace and forgiveness is displeasing to our Father in Heaven and His Son, Jesus Christ. Elder Packer cautioned, "Some worry endlessly over missions that were missed, or marriages that did not turn out, or babies that did not arrive, or children that seem lost, or dreams unfulfilled, or because age limits what they can do. I do not think it pleases the Lord when we worry because we think we never do enough or that what we do is never good enough. Some needlessly carry a heavy burden of guilt which could be removed through confession and repentance."[97]

Sin causes pain, and through blatant sin certain opportunities can be lost forever. But those who transgress should never be made to feel that all they can now offer to the Lord is feeble, worthless service. To communicate to repentant souls that they will be spiritually inadequate the rest of their lives is not only callous but wrong. Elder Scott said: "If you have repented from serious transgression and *mistakenly believe that you will always be a second-class citizen* in the kingdom of God, *learn that is not true.* . . . Find encouragement in the lives of Alma the Younger and the sons of Mosiah. They were tragically wicked. Yet their full repentance and service qualified them to be considered as noble as righteous Captain Moroni. To you who have sincerely repented yet continue to feel the burden of guilt, realize that to continue to suffer for sins when there has been proper repentance and forgiveness of the Lord is prompted by the master of deceit. Lucifer will encourage you to continue to relive the details of past mistakes, knowing that such thoughts can hamper your progress. Thus he attempts to tie strings to the mind and body so that he can manipulate you like a puppet to discourage personal achievement."[98]

The Gospel of Work[99] and Wasted Time

Why might an individual deny himself of the Lord's mercy and forgiveness? Why might a parent, a teacher, or a leader be apt to do the same thing to the sinner? Perhaps it is a sincere yet misplaced desire to avoid giving license to sin. Bruce C. Hafen cautioned that at times there are "some Church members [who] feel entitled to 'a few free ones' as they sow their wild oats and walk constantly along the edge of transgression. Or they believe that repentance requires little more than saying they are

---

97 In Conference Report, Oct. 2004.

98 In Conference Report, Oct. 2000.

99 See chapter heading for 2 Thessalonians 3.

sorry. Constant emphasis on the availability of forgiveness can be counterproductive in such cases, suggesting—wrongly—that they can 'live it up' now and repent easily later without harmful consequences." Elder Hafen then instructively warned, "Despite these reasons for caution, the blessing of *making the Atonement more central to our lives outweighs any associated risks. When we habitually understate the Atonement's broad meaning, we do more harm than leaving one another without comforting reassurances*--for some may simply drop out of the race, weighed down beyond the breaking point with self-doubt and spiritual fatigue."[100]

Teaching youth how to properly understand the meaning of forgiveness can be a rewarding yet daunting task. Likewise, teachers, leaders, and parents must help those in their stewardships to avoid wasting time and putting off spiritual change. "Yea, I would that ye would come forth and harden not your hearts any longer," said Alma,

> For behold, now is the time and the day of your salvation; and therefore, if ye will repent and harden not your hearts, immediately shall the great plan of redemption be brought about unto you. For behold, this life is the time for men to prepare to meet God; yea, behold the day of this life is the day for men to perform their labors. And now, as I said unto you before, as ye have had so many witnesses, therefore, I beseech of you that ye do not procrastinate the day of your repentance until the end; for after this day of life, which is given us to prepare for eternity, behold, if we do not improve our time while in this life, then cometh the night of darkness wherein there can be no labor performed. (Alma 34:31–35)

---

100 "Beauty for Ashes," *Liahona*, Apr. 1997, 39.

There is a lesson in the parable of the laborers in the vineyard as we contemplate principles regarding sloth, procrastination, and wasted time. In this parable there are laborers who come to work—some for the entire day, others for part of the day, and others for just one hour. In the end, however, all receive the same reward (see Matthew 20). Those who worked in the vineyard all day were fortunate enough to get work early on, fortunate to be able to have the opportunity to earn a wage. Those who came late had waited and watched for an opportunity to work but had found none until the master of the vineyard found and hired them. When one contemplates the murmuring response of those who labored all day in the vineyard, their expression is ironic at best and absolutely absurd at worst. If we were to liken the parable unto ourselves as active members of the Church, what would we in actuality be saying? "Oh, how difficult it has been to keep the commandments. Oh, how horrible it has been to be in the covenant relationship. Oh, the drudgery of having true happiness and peace my whole life. Oh, the burden of having the joy of the companionship of the Holy Ghost. I am so envious of those who have labored but one hour. I wish I could be like them—the darkness, the depression— oh, the exquisite misery I could have had during my life, the horrible pain of happiness!" One would expect that a lifetime enjoyment of peace and spiritual prosperity would be in and of itself its own reward, regardless of even greater rewards in the next life. When we truly contemplate this unappreciative attitude toward a righteous life, we are almost inclined to ask if the complaining all-day-long laborer was truly converted in the first place? Was he just going through the motions? Were his service and commitment to the kingdom based on reasons other than those approved by Father in Heaven?

Perhaps there are those who labor in the vineyard and feel they are doing the heavens some great favor. It is as though commitment to the kingdom is inextricably linked to a life of oppression, drudgery, and discontent due to the arduous walk of

Christlike living. Harry Emerson Fosdick perceptively observed: "Some Christians carry their religion on their backs. It is a packet of beliefs and practices which they must bear. At times it grows heavy and they would willingly lay it down, but that would mean a break with old traditions, so they shoulder it again. But real Christians do not carry their religion, their religion carries them. It is not weight; it is wings. It lifts them up, it sees them over hard places, it makes the universe seem friendly, life purposeful, hope real, sacrifice worthwhile. It sets them free from fear, futility, discouragement, and sin—the great enslavers of men's souls. You can know a real Christian, when you see him, by his buoyancy."

If the penny each laborer received represented the celestial glory of eternal life, perhaps these murmurers would be shocked to realize that they might not, in the end, even want the reward for which they labored so zealously. It's worth quoting President Marion G. Romney again: "Service is not something we endure on this earth so we can earn the right to live in the celestial kingdom. Service is the very fiber of which an exalted life in the celestial kingdom is made." Surely the focus of these disgruntled laborers is on the late-arriving laborers who seemingly receive the same reward with little effort. However, it's important to note the fact that the late-comers' standing idle in the marketplace does not mean they were lazy, complacent, or even rebellious. When asked why they were idle, these workers responded, "Because no man hath hired us." These workers were in the marketplace, they wanted to be hired, they were willing to work, but none was available at the time. Nevertheless they waited; diligently, patiently, they waited for work, no matter how much or how little. They did not go home or to the pool hall to pass the time.

Surely these types should be credited for enduring the uncertainty of unemployment and for their unwavering vigilance. Surely their long-working counterparts should respect them for their fortitude. Anyone with experience in real living knows the horrible monotony and depressing curse of not being "anxiously engaged in a good cause." Work is not drudgery. As the following quote illustrates, work is a blessing, the lack of it a curse. "If you are poor, work. . . . If you are happy, work. Idleness gives room for doubts and fears. If disappointments come, keep right on working. If sorrow overwhelms you, . . . work. . . . When faith falters and reason fails, just work. When dreams are shattered and hope seems dead, work. Work as if your life were in peril. It really is. No matter what ails you, work. Work faithfully. . . . Work is the greatest remedy available for both mental and physical afflictions."[101] What a blessing it is to be able to work all the day long, and what a blessing for those who've been unable, for whatever reason, when they at last are able to join those already engaged in the cause. We would hope that those fortunate enough to have worked all day in the vineyard would look with compassion on those who truly wanted work but lacked the opportunity. How fortunate are we, indeed, that the merciful Master of the vineyard blesses us even for our righteous desires and our willingness to work when given the chance.

Conclusion

Our Father in Heaven is a God of forgiveness, and through repentance sin can be forgiven. Despite the availability of God's forgiveness, however, sin can cause an individual to loose opportunities forever. As parents, teachers, and leaders in the Church, we must be careful never to give those in our stewardship the "license to sin." However, and more importantly, we cannot understate the power and ability of Christ's Atonement to change, redeem, and bless. No, mercy cannot rob justice (see Alma 42:25), but mercy can and does overpower justice (see Alma 34:15). We must not be afraid or ashamed to speak of

---

101 Korsaren, *The Forbes Scrapbook of Thoughts on the Business of Life*, New York: Forbes Inc., 1968, 427; in J. Richard Clarke, "The Value of Work," *Ensign*, May 1982, 78.

mercy, forgiveness, grace, and God's divine love:[102] "And now, beloved, marvel not that I tell you these things; for why not speak of the atonement of Christ" (Ether 4:12).

In the end, each of us needs the Atonement. No one can save and redeem themselves. Each of us inevitably sins to some degree (see Romans 3:23). We all fall short and miss out on certain opportunities. Will we squander the precious gift of forgiveness Christ has offered us? Or will we come down into the depths of humility and be accepting of His great atoning sacrifice? "Are you struggling with some sin or weakness?" asked Elder M. Russell Ballard. "It can be something as simple as not having the will power to rise in the morning early enough to have time for scripture study and prayer. It can be something so powerful, such as Internet pornography or lack of moral self-control, that you feel like you have been pulled down into an abyss and there is no hope for you. Do you find yourself hating what you are doing but not able to find the will power to turn away from it? Then reach out and humble yourself. The Lord's enabling power is sufficient to change your heart, to turn your life, to purge your soul. But you must make the first move, which is to humble yourself and realize that only in God can you find deliverance."[103] May we all humbly and gratefully recognize the wonderful gift of repentance in our own lives and in the lives of those we love and serve. May we continually remember that the Savior's grace and love really are "sufficient

---

102 See Neal A. Maxwell, "Jesus of Nazareth, Savior and King," *Ensign,* May 1976, 26; Russell M. Nelson, "These . . . Were Our Examples," *Ensign,* Nov. 1991, 61; Gardner H. Russell, "Touching the Hearts of Less-Active Members," *Ensign,* Nov. 1986, 28; Victor L. Brown, "A Lifetime of Learning," *Ensign,* Nov. 1989, 77; Robert E. Wells, "The Beatitudes: Pattern for Coming unto Christ," *Ensign,* Dec. 1987, 10; W. Mack Lawrence, "Sunday Worship Service," *Ensign,* May 1991, 30; Robert J. Whetten, "True Followers," *Ensign,* May 1999, 30.

103 "Be Strong in the Lord, and in the Power of His Might" (fireside for young adults, Mar. 3, 2002).

to own, redeem, and to justify,"[104] not only for those who have labored all day long but for those who receive the opportunity to labor whenever it comes.

104 "I Stand All Amazed," *Hymns,* no. 193.

Signs of the Times: The Multiple Fulfillment of Joel 2:28–32

"This know also, that in the last days perilous times shall come."
—2 Timothy 3:1

"It has always been surprising to me that after . . . one hundred and sixty-five . . . years of Church history, our people have made few, if any, serious attempts to expound the book of Joel and determine its full meaning. It stands to reason that the prophecy must be of great importance, or Moroni would not have quoted parts of it to the young prophet."[105]

ELDER DALLIN H. OAKS OF the Quorum of the Twelve Apostles once observed, "Many of the prophecies and doctrinal passages in the scriptures have multiple meanings." [106] He specifically mentioned the well-known prophecy in the book of Joel, which states, among other things, that the Lord would pour out his spirit upon all flesh and that sons and daughters would prophesy (see Joel 2:28). Prophets both ancient and modern have commented on the fulfillment of this prophecy, which has now reached a zenith in its fulfillment in these last days.

105 FARMS [Spring 1995] vol. 4, no. 1, 280–81.
106 Dallin H. Oaks, "Scripture Reading and Revelation," *Ensign*, Jan. 1995, 8.

The realization of this fulfillment can and should be a source of excitement and hope for all Latter-day Saints, especially those who are burdened with anxiety over the ever-increasing onslaught of wickedness and depravity in these last days.

Conditions in the World Today as Foretold by Prophets

In order to more fully appreciate the prophecy in Joel 2, it is important to first understand the context of the times in which this prophecy would be fulfilled. As part of the Restoration of the gospel of Jesus Christ and the ushering in of the dispensation of the fullness of times, we learn the sobering truth that as spiritual light would increase, so would spiritual darkness. Prophets both ancient and modern have described in detail the ever-increasing evil that would characterize the last days, specifically the times immediately preceding the Second Coming of the Savior. Illustratively, Brigham Young observed: "It was revealed to me in the commencement of this Church, that the Church would spread, prosper, grow and extend, and that in proportion to the spread of the Gospel among the nations of the earth, so would the power of Satan rise."[107] Elder Boyd K. Packer likewise observed: "We live in troubled times—very troubled times. We hope, we pray for better days. But that is not to be. The prophecies tell us that. We will not as a people, as families, or as individuals be exempt from the trials to come."[108] Additionally, in D&C 1:35 the Lord, through the prophet Joseph Smith, warns: "The hour is not yet, but is nigh at hand, *when peace shall be taken from the earth, and the devil shall have power* over his own dominion." Elder M. Russell Ballard has recently declared that this prophecy, given in 1831, has now been fulfilled.[109] We know that peace again be restored one day as Christ's millennial reign commences; however, it is sobering to realize that we now live in the time foretold by prophets when "the heavens shall be

107 *Discourses of Brigham Young,* 72.
108 Boyd K. Packer, in Conference Report, April 2000, 8.
109 See Elder Ballard, CES Broadcast, 3 March 2002.

darkened, and a veil of darkness shall cover the earth; and the heavens shall shake, and also the earth; and great tribulations shall be among the children of men, but my people will I preserve; And righteousness will I send down out of heaven; and truth will I send forth out of the earth, to bear testimony of mine Only Begotten; his resurrection from the dead; yea, and also the resurrection of all men; and righteousness and truth will I cause to sweep the earth as with a flood" (Moses 7:61–62).

It is interesting to note that Elder Packer specifically warns that even Latter-day Saints will not be exempt from the trials to come. Because of this predicament, modern prophets have consistently taught that as the last days unfold, members of the Church will need to continually increase their efforts to lay hold on righteousness. Elder Bruce R. McConkie taught that "conditions in the world are not going to get better" during these last days.

They are going to get worse until the coming of the Son of Man, which is the end of the world, when the wicked will be destroyed. The world is going to get worse, and the faithful portion of the Church, at least, is going to get better. The day is coming, more than ever has been the case in the past, when we will be under the obligation of making a choice, of standing up for the Church, of adhering to its precepts and teachings and principles, of taking the counsel that comes from the apostles and prophets whom God has placed to teach the doctrine and bear witness to the world. *The day is coming when this will be more necessary than has ever been the case in our day or at any time in our dispensation.*[110]

Similarly, President James E. Faust described the specific increases in righteousness that living in the last days would necessitate: "Great challenges lie ahead unless the power of faith, judgment, honesty, decency, self-control, and character increases proportionately to compensate for this expansion of secular

---

110 Bruce R. McConkie, "Be Valiant in the Fight of Faith," *Ensign*, Nov. 1974, 35.

knowledge. Without moral progress, stimulated by faith in God, immorality in all its forms will proliferate and strangle goodness and human decency."[111] We will be tested as never before in a word that calls good evil and evil good. In a poignant address given to the Church Educational System in August 2001, Elder Henry B. Eyring gave this vivid description of the situation we are facing:

The world in which our students choose spiritual life or death is changing rapidly. When their older brothers and sisters return to visit the same schools and campuses they attended, they find a radically different moral climate. The language in the hallways and the locker rooms has coarsened. Clothing is less modest. Pornography has moved into the open. *Tolerance for wickedness has not only increased,* but much of what was called wrong is no longer condemned at all and may, even by our students, be admired. Parents and administrators have in many cases bent to the pressures coming from a shifting world to retreat from moral standards once widely accepted. *The spiritual strength sufficient for our youth to stand firm just a few years ago will soon not be enough.* Many of them are remarkable in their spiritual maturity and in their faith. But even the best of them are sorely tested. And *the testing will become more severe.*[112]

Not only will the testing get more severe, but the increases in depravity and lewdness will never return to the lower levels of the past. The only defense we have against the onslaught is self-defense, or, as Elder Holland observed, self-control:

Recently I read an author who said: 'Our leisure, even our play, is a matter of serious concern. [That is because] there is no neutral ground in the universe: every square inch, every split second, is claimed by God and counterclaimed by Satan.' I believe that to be absolutely true, and no such claiming and counterclaiming anywhere is more crucial and conspicuous than that being waged for the minds and morals, the personal purity

111 James E. Faust, in Conference Report, April 2000, 20.
112 Henry B. Eyring, CES Address, August 2001.

of the young. Brethren, *part of my warning voice tonight is that this will only get worse.* It seems the door to permissiveness, the door to lewdness and vulgarity and obscenity swings only one way. It only opens farther and farther; it never seems to swing back. Individuals can choose to close it, but it is certain, historically speaking, that public appetite and public policy will not close it. No, in the moral realm the only real control you have is self-control.[113]

Even President Hinckley warned of this perilous time of ever increasing darkness and the blurring of the lines between right and wrong: "But wonderful as this time is, it is fraught with peril. Evil is all about us. It is attractive and tempting and in so many cases successful. . . . We live in a season when fierce men do terrible and despicable things." He continues, "We live in a season of wickedness, pornography, immorality. All of the sins of Sodom and Gomorrah haunt our society. Our young people have never faced a greater challenge. We have never seen more clearly the lecherous face of evil."[114]

Clearly these are dangerous times in which we live. It is difficult enough for us as Latter-day Saints to witness the frightening onslaught of evil in the word today and to contemplate the ever-increasing amount we will inevitably face in the future, but what adds to our anxiety is the thought that levels of righteousness sufficient in years past will no longer be adequate and that we will continually have to do more and more to combat the evil. But we know that God is merciful and gracious. We know that though we may feel like a temptation or trial is beyond our ability to withstand, He will, "with the temptation also make a way to escape, that [we] may be able to bear it" (1 Cor. 10:13). We know for certain that He will prepare a way for us to accomplish those things that he has commanded us (1 Nephi 3:7). And so it in these last days. God expects more out of us for sure, but He has also provided and will continue to provide compensatory

---

113 Jeffery R. Holland, CR, October 2000.
114 Gordon B. Hinckley, "Living in the Fulness of Times," *Ensign,* November, 2001, 5–6.

and enabling power to those that love Him with all their might, mind, and strength. In the prophesy of Joel we learn not only about what we will need to do, but comfortingly, what God will do to counteract the flood of evil being poured out in these last days.

The Prophecy

One of the minor prophets in the Old Testament, Joel's contribution to the canon is small in quantity, but enormous in its import. Only three chapters in length, the book of Joel focuses almost entirely on events preceding the Second Coming. The centerpiece of the prophecy is the second chapter, specifically the last six verses or so.

And it shall come to pass afterward, *that* I will pour out my spirit upon all flesh; and your sons and your daughters shall prophesy, your old men shall dream dreams, your young men shall see visions: And also upon the servants and upon the handmaids in those days will I pour out my spirit. And I will shew wonders in the heavens and in the earth, blood, and fire, and pillars of smoke. The sun shall be turned into darkness, and the moon into blood, before the great and the terrible day of the Lord come. And it shall come to pass, that whosoever shall call on the name of the Lord shall be delivered: for in mount Zion and in Jerusalem shall be deliverance, as the Lord hath said, and in the remnant whom the Lord shall call. (Joel 2:28–32)

Three themes are evident in these verses: 1) wonders in the heavens, 2) deliverance for the faithful, and 3) the outpouring of the Spirit on all flesh. Although each of these themes is of interest and importance, the third deserves particular attention.

Ancient Commentary

That the early Apostles knew of Joel's prophesy is abundantly clear from the book of Acts. After the tremendous outpouring of the Spirit on the day of Pentecost, Peter seized the opportunity to identify the workings of the Spirit by likening their experience to the scriptural explanation provided by Joel:

> But this is that which was spoken by the prophet
> Joel; And it shall come to pass in the last days,
> saith God, I will pour out of my Spirit upon all
> flesh: and your sons and your daughters shall
> prophesy, and your young men shall see visions,
> and your old men shall dream dreams. (Acts
> 2:16–17)

Those without modern prophets and continuing revelation might insist that Joel's prophecy was fulfilled on this occasion, but Moroni's visit to Joseph Smith in 1823 provides additional insight. During the visit, Moroni quoted several scriptures from the Old and New Testaments, then, Joseph related: "He also quoted the second chapter of Joel, from the twenty-eighth verse to the last. He also said that this was *not yet fulfilled, but was soon to be*" (JS–H 1:41; emphasis added).

Although the fulfillment of the prophecy of Joel seems to be implied in Peter's assertion, there is no explicit statement that such is the case. It could be argued that Peter is merely mentioning this so as to "liken" the scriptures unto those in his day. Elder McConkie's insight is helpful: "Peter's application to his day of a yet-to-be fulfilled prophecy was proper because the passage teaches there would be visions, dreams, revelations, and spiritual outpourings among God's people. There was thus a partial and incomplete fulfillment in Peter's day, with the great pre-millennial manifestations being reserved for the appointed time."[115] Suffice it to say that, in 1823 at least, this prophesy was not yet fulfilled.

Ten years later a revelation in the Doctrine and Covenants seems to indicate that the fulfillment of this prophecy was still in the future:

For ye have sinned against me a very grievous sin, in that ye have not considered the great commandment in all things, that I have given unto you concerning the *building of mine house*; For the preparation wherewith I design to prepare mine apostles to

---

115 *DNTC*, 2:35.

prune my vineyard for the last time, that I may bring to pass my strange act, *that I may pour out my Spirit upon all flesh.* (D&C 95:3-4)

It is worth noting the sequence of events prior to the fulfillment of Joel's prophecy: the building of the Kirtland Temple, the preparation of the Apostles (probably the endowment), and the bringing to pass of God's strange act, which act, as will be explained later, is likely the outpouring of the Spirit upon all flesh. And this outpouring, as of 1833, was still yet to come in its fullness. It is interesting to note the connection between this prophecy regarding the building of the Kirtland Temple as it relates to the other temples that would be built in the future. It could be said that temple building is directly correlated with, and indeed is one of the very means for, the outpouring of the Spirit upon all flesh.

Modern Commentary

Over 140 years later, President Joseph Fielding Smith gave some interesting commentary regarding several of the signs contained in this prophesy in Joel 2. Among other things, he stated the following: "Thus, the work of the Lord is advancing, and all these things are signs of the near approach of our Lord. *The words of the prophets are rapidly being fulfilled*, but it is done on such natural principles that most of us fail to see it. Wonders in heaven and in the earth should be seen, and there should be fire, blood, and pillars of smoke. *Eventually* the sun is to be turned into darkness and the moon as blood, and then shall come the great and dreadful day of the Lord. *Some of these signs have been given; some are yet to come.*"[116] By the end of the twentieth century, the time for the fulfillment of this prophecy in Joel was shaping up .

Then, in the October 2001 conference, President Hinckley made the following statement at the outset of the proceedings on Saturday morning: "The era in which we live is the fulness

116 Joseph Fielding Smith, "Signs of the Times," *Ensign*, July 1971, 33.

of times spoken of in the scriptures, when God has brought together all of the elements of previous dispensations. From the day that He and His Beloved Son manifested themselves to the boy Joseph, there has been a tremendous cascade of enlightenment poured out upon the world. The hearts of men have turned to their fathers in fulfillment of the words of Malachi. *The vision of Joel has been fulfilled* wherein he declared . . ." President Hinckley then quoted Joel 2:28–32. Many individuals that day, myself included, were filled with wonder and amazement as a prophet of God shared his conviction that this ancient prophecy, highlighted by the angel Moroni over 170 years ago, had now been fulfilled. It is breathtaking to be living in such a time when such events are unfolding right before our eyes. Joseph Smith once commented that many of the ancients "prophets, priests and kings have dwelt with peculiar delight" upon thoughts of the culminating events of these last days, and that they "have looked forward *with joyful anticipation* to the day in which we live; and fired with heavenly and joyful anticipations they have sung and written and prophesied of this our day; but they died without the sight; we are the favored people that God has made choice of to bring about the Latter-day glory."[117] And isn't it interesting that the single greatest season of temple building in the history of this world (1999–2001) occurred *precisely* at the time a prophet of God said this prophesy had been fulfilled?

What connection does the fulfillment of this prophesy in Joel have with the ever-increasing tide of evil we've learned would wash over the earth in these troubled times? As stated earlier, our Father in Heaven will not leave us alone to combat the escalation of evil. He not only expects more out of us but will give compensatory help. Within the prophesy of Joel, and its corresponding fulfillment, one sees the very keys of divine help for us in these last days. In 2004, Elder Henry B. Eyring of the Quorum of the Twelve further amplified President

117 Joseph Smith, HC 4:609 -10.

Hinckley's 2001 prophetic announcement of the fulfillment of the Joel prophesy.[118] In a Church Educational System satellite broadcast, Elder Eyring focused almost his entire remarks on the Joel prophesy. Elder Eyring explained that "these words and this prophecy are for every young person you love. And they are for you and for me." He then quoted Joel 2:27–32, just as President Hinckley and Moroni had done, and gave this sobering and thrilling instruction:

> This is not poetry, nor is it allegory; it is description of reality as it will be. Some of it will happen so gradually that you may not notice it. Some has already begun across the Church and we may not have seen the blessing developing, or at least we may not have done what we must to help the Lord with these miracles. That scripture does not say that your sons and your daughters *may* claim the gift of prophecy by the Spirit. It says that they will. It doesn't say that your young men *may* see visions. It says that they will. And it will come because the Lord will pour out His Spirit upon all flesh. Not only will the youth you love and serve have the Spirit poured out on them, but so will the people around them and those who lead them.
>
> One of the dangers of the times we are passing into is that we might be tempted to lower our expectations for ourselves and for those young people we serve. As the world darkens, even a partial conversion and a few spiritual experiences may seem more and more remarkable, compared to the world. We might be tempted to expect less. The Lord has given another signal, clear and

---

118 Elder Henry B. Eyring, "Raising Expectations", CES Satellite Broadcast, Aug 2004

powerful. It is that we can expect more, not less, of youth.

How comforting to know that not only has the prophesy in Joel been fulfilled but that it will continue to be fulfilled again and again as the Lord "pours out his spirit" in order to bless and strengthen the Saints so that they might endure the tremendous trials of the last days. Elder Eyring gave a caution, however, and warned that not everyone would be so protected: "The Spirit will be poured out, but it will wash over some and fall to the ground and fail to make a difference. The Spirit will be poured out, but choices must be made in faith to receive spiritual power. . . . Whether or not that outpouring of the Spirit on all flesh brings prophecies and visions and safety to the young people we love will depend upon their choices."

Elder Eyring then taught parents, teachers, and leaders that they can make a difference in the way youth lay hold upon the promised blessings as prophesied by Joel. Instructively, he reminded us: "You know the choices they must make that matter most. So you can make it far more likely that they will choose what will let them claim a constant companionship of the Spirit. That is what they *can* have. That is what they *must* have." He continues: "It begins with expectations, yours and theirs. If you expect little, they will feel your lack of faith in them and in the Lord's promised outpouring of the Spirit. If you communicate, by word or action or even by your tone of voice, that you doubt their spiritual capacity, they will doubt it. If you see in them the potential Joel describes, they will at least have the chance to see it in themselves. Your choices of what you expect will have powerful effect on their choices of what to expect of themselves."

As parents, teachers, and leaders, we should be comforted to know that we are not alone in our efforts to teach and bless the youth of the Church. Many years ago, while working for the Church Educational System as a field coordinator, I had the opportunity to visit the classes of a number of wonderful and dedicated volunteer early morning seminary teachers. The work was rewarding and humbling, to say the least. I can personally testify to the truthfulness of Elder Eyring's words as I saw his promises evidenced in the lives of both teachers and students. I can also testify that such experiences usually occur "on such natural principles that most of us fail to see [them]," as President Joseph Fielding Smith said earlier. One such experience involved a particular teacher, one of her students, and their class—all of whom experienced the promised outpouring of the Spirit as prophesied by Joel. With the teacher's permission and having changed the names for purposes of confidentiality, I'd like to share portions of a letter she sent me. Her experience and that of her students is inspiring and helps us to see the "natural" yet priceless outcomes that occur in the lives of those who "choose" to take hold of the Spirit being poured out. She shares the following:

> I have learned many things this seminary year and have had many successes, but none more rewarding than watching the growth of one particular student of mine. His name is Mike, and he is a seventeen-year-old freshman. He has had lots of setbacks in his "educational career" and is in special needs classes to help him with his reading. He has trouble with phonics and pronunciations, and probably reads on a second- or third-grade level. At the beginning of the school year, he was a quiet, shy young man who did not particularly want to be in seminary. Before school started, his mother told me it would be best not to ask him to read out loud because he gets embarrassed and feels awkward. I originally put the kids in pairs to work together so he wouldn't always have to be the last one to complete assignments. After a few weeks of seminary, I had the kids do some reading. I told

them when it came to their turn, and they didn't feel like reading, just to say "pass." When we got to Mike, he told me he would like to read. Mike takes a very long time to work through the words, but because the seminary kids have a special bond, no one pressures him or makes him feel awkward. A couple months later, I told his mother how pleased I was that Mike was willing to read in class. She conveyed to me that Mike expressed to her that he didn't mind reading in seminary because the kids were his friends and he knew they wouldn't make fun of him. He doesn't get that luxury at school.

As the months have progressed, Mike has really found his confidence. With encouragement, he has lost seventy pounds this year, become very outgoing, and has improved his grades dramatically. His family have only been Church members a few years, so this is their first seminary experience. Last month in seminary, we talked of Christ instituting the sacrament among the Nephites. I asked him when he planned on blessing the sacrament. He indicated that he would be too nervous and didn't think he would be able to do it right. After talking with the branch president and being found worthy, Mike received a copy of the sacrament prayers and started working on them. He practiced each morning in seminary, and last Sunday, we all felt each word as Mike blessed the sacrament for the first time. He did a beautiful job, pronouncing each word perfectly and with confidence. I thanked him for being a worthy priesthood holder and doing something for me that I could not do myself.

"Thanks be to God, which giveth us the victory through our Lord Jesus Christ" (1 Corinthians 15:57). "Thanks be unto God for his unspeakable gift" (2 Corinthians 9:15). And thanks be to God, our Father in Heaven, for pouring out His Spirit in these last days.

Conclusion

We live in times of great spiritual danger. Wickedness, evil, and depravity will continue to worsen as we draw closer to the Second Coming. Our Father in Heaven, however, has not, and will not, leave us alone to falter. He has brought forth and will continue to bring forth compensatory powers that will enable us, our children, and those we love to withstand and overcome the tidal wave of darkness that will be unleashed upon the earth in these last days. President Boyd K. Packer taught of this reality in a World Wide Leadership Training session in 2010:

> In order to live by the Spirit and teach by the Spirit, we can do much better than we are doing. We face a world now that is terrifying in its influence upon the Saints and their families. The adversary rejoices. *But we need not be discouraged.* The Lord said, "And it shall come to pass in the last days, saith God, I will pour out of my Spirit upon all flesh: and your sons and your daughters shall prophesy, and your young men shall see visions, and your old men shall dream dreams" (Joel 2:28). It is a spiritual work that we are about, and a spiritual work must be guided by the Spirit. In our day and age there is always the danger of establishing the Church without establishing the gospel. It is not enough. We need to have the Church in the lives of the members and the gospel established in the hearts of the members.

If we are not careful, our members are kept so
busy concerning themselves with programs and
procedures and buildings and budgets that the
spiritual testimony is not firmly planted.[119]

How comforting it is to know that this divine mercy and
help will be available to us if we so choose. It is true that without
our best efforts and ever increasing determination, we will not be
able to stand. But additionally, we need the aid of heaven—and
help is on its way!

Years ago President Hinckley gave this instruction and
blessing: "You cannot expect to do it alone. You need heaven's
help in rearing heaven's child—your child, who is also the child
of his or her Heavenly Father. O God, our Eternal Father, bless
the parents to teach with love and patience and encouragement
those who are most precious, the children who have come from
Thee, that together they might be safeguarded and directed for
good and, in the process of growth, bring blessings to the world
of which they will be a part, I pray In the name of Jesus Christ,
amen."[120]

---

119 2010 Worldwide Leadership Training Meeting.

120 Gordon B. Hinckley, "Bring Up a Child in the Way He Should Go,"
Ensign, Nov. 1993, 60.

SECTION 3

"From Everlasting to Everlasting":
Reflections on Eternity

Eternities Past: Retroactive Time and Premortal Redemption

---

*"And behold, Enoch saw the day of the coming of the Son
of Man, even in the flesh; and his soul rejoiced, saying: The
Righteous is lifted up, and the Lamb is slain from the foundation
of the world; and through faith I am in the bosom of the Father,
and behold, Zion is with me." (Moses 7:47)*

THE BOOK OF MORMON OFFERS a priceless addition to the
Christian world's understanding of the Atonement. Within its
pages, we are given a description of "an *infinite* atonement" (see
2 Nephi 9:7; 25:16; Alma 34:9–14; emphasis added). Though
there are many instances of this, we will mention just one for
present purposes. The scriptures, both ancient and modern, are
replete with teachings regarding the retroactive nature of Christ's
Atonement (see Revelation 5; Alma 39 chapter heading; Mosiah
4:6–7; Mosiah 3:13; Jarom 1:11; Mosiah 16:6; Moses 7:47).
This retroactive nature is in part what qualifies it as "an infinite
atonement." Book of Mormon prophets preached about the
Atonement and encouraged the people to believe in Christ "as
though he had already come" (Mosiah 3:13) Thus, many years
before the coming of Christ in the meridian of time, individuals
such as Alma the Younger and Lamoni were able to exercise faith

in the Atonement and access its power to receive a remission of sins and a mighty change of heart. In fact, scripture attests that the retroactive power of the Atonement stretches back even into the premortal existence. God set up a "preparatory redemption" (Alma 13:3) for His children. Interestingly, since the power of the Atonement extends back to the premortal existence, it would stand to reason that all specific aspects of the Atonement would be operative as well.

One of the precious and glorious truths we learn from the Book of Mormon is the nature of certain conditions in the premortal existence. Spirit sons and daughters of God had agency in the life before and were free to "choose good or evil" (Alma 13:3). We are told that some exercised "exceedingly great faith" (Alma 13:3) in that realm. It is interesting to note that even though they were in God's presence, they needed faith. Obviously we would need to have faith in the future of God's plan, which would be enacted on the earth, but there is another reason they needed faith.

The fact that we could choose evil is another way of saying we could sin. This may, at first glance, seem at odds with the scriptural declaration that "no unclean thing can dwell with God" (1 Nephi 10:21; Moses 6:57). It would appear intuitive, though, that if we really had the ability to choose, we could certainly choose poorly. Joseph Fielding Smith put it this way: "God gave his children their free agency even in the spirit world, by which the individual spirits had the privilege, just as men have here, of *choosing the good and rejecting the evil*, or [in other words] partaking of the evil *to suffer the consequences of their sins.* Because of this, some even there were more faithful than others in keeping the commandments of the Lord."[121] It is true that no unclean thing can dwell with God. The key is in the definition of the word *dwell*, meaning "to remain there permanently." Thus, individuals bound for either telestial or terrestrial glory—even

---

121 Joseph Fielding Smith, *Doctrines of Salvation,* 3 vols., ed. Bruce R. Mc-Conkie (Salt Lake City: Deseret Book, 1954), 1:58–59; emphasis added.

those mortals on earth who commit the unpardonable sin and become sons of perdition—will be brought back temporarily into God's presence for the Final Judgment.[122] So it would appear that we *can* sin and remain in God's presence—temporarily.

So why would we need faith in the premortal realm? The answer is gloriously profound yet plain and simple. Consider this verse from the Doctrine and Covenants: "Every spirit of man was innocent in the beginning; and God having redeemed man from the fall, men became again, in their infant state, innocent before God" (D&C 93:38). It is interesting to note the dual innocence mentioned here. Elder Bruce R. McConkie gave this explanation regarding the meaning of these words: "There is no such thing as original sin as such is defined in the creeds of Christendom. Such a concept denies the efficacy of the atonement. Our revelation says: 'Every spirit of man was innocent in the beginning'— *meaning that spirits started out in a state of purity and innocence in preexistence*—'and God having redeemed man from the fall, men became *again*, in their infant state, innocent before God' (D&C 93:38)--meaning that all children start their mortal probation *in purity and innocence because of the atonement.*"[123]

We exercised faith in the premortal realm, and, more importantly, we exercised faith in the Atonement of Jesus Christ to the extent that we were able to receive a remission of the sins committed in that first estate as well. Orson Pratt explained that "Jesus [offered] himself as an acceptable offering and sacrifice before the Father to atone for the sins of His brethren, committed, not only in the second, but also in the first estate."[124] No wonder Alma calls it a "preparatory redemption" (Alma 13:3). In his book, *The Infinite Atonement,* Elder Tad R. Callister summarizes this truth: "We began our spirit existence in an innocent state, meaning we were pure and free from sin. . . . Through the

122 See 2 Nephi 9:15.
123 "The Salvation of Little Children," *Ensign,* Apr. 1977, 4; emphasis added.
124 *The Seer,* Salt Lake City: Eugene Wagner, 1901, 54.

Atonement of Jesus Christ and his redeeming powers, we were likewise born innocent into mortality—untainted and unstained from our premortal sins."[125]

Apparently this condition of innocence applies to every person who comes to earth as a mortal. It stands to reason, then, that every person on earth, whether of high or low station, whether good or bad, has applied the atoning blood of Christ and received a remission of sin, if only in that premortal existence. Joseph Fielding Smith explained that "in the beginning of this mortal life—no matter how faithful, or how valiant, or otherwise, we were in that spirit world—when we come into this world, we come into it innocent as far as this world is concerned, just as we were innocent in the other world in the beginning. Every child—I don't care where it is born; I don't care what its color— that is born into this world comes into it innocent in its infant state."[126]

The reality of the possibility of sin and the associated operational nature of the Atonement in the premortal existence is portrayed beautifully in the hymn, "O Thou, Before the World Began":

O thou, before the world began,
Ordained a sacrifice for man,
And by th'eternal Spirit made
An off'ring in the sinner's stead;
Our everlasting Priest art thou,
Pleading thy death for sinners now.

Thy off'ring still continues new
Before the righteous Father's view.
Thyself the Lamb forever slain;
Thy priesthood doth unchanged remain.
Thy years, O God, can never fail,
Nor thy blest work within the veil.

125 *The Infinite Atonement*, 79.
126 *Doctrines of Salvation*, 2:51.

Oh, that our faith may never move
But stand unshaken as thy love,
Sure evidence of things unseen;
Now let it pass the years between
And view thee bleeding on the tree:
My Lord, my God, who dies for me.[127]

Justification and Sanctification in the Premortal Existence

If we received a remission of sins in that premortal world, then we can safely conclude that justification was an operative principle. Alma confirmed this when he said that "many being called and prepared *from the foundation of the world* according to the foreknowledge of God" partook of Christ's redemptive power "on account of their exceeding faith [in His Atonement] and *repentance,* and their righteousness before God, they *choosing to repent* and work righteousness rather than to perish" (Alma 13:3, 10). Section 93 of the Doctrine and Covenants harmonizes with this, since we became "innocent again," meaning free of sin.

Sanctification was also possible prior to our mortal sojourn, however strange this may sound, since sanctification is a process—one that some think only occurs on earth. Several passages of scripture relating to the salvation of little children can help us to understand this concept: "But behold, I say unto you, that little children are redeemed from the foundation of the world through mine Only Begotten" (D&C 29:46). This verse confirms what we already know—that children come to earth redeemed through Christ's Atonement applied in the premortal existence. They are innocent *again* and they are "whole from the foundation of the world" (Moses 6:54). These verses do not explicitly mention sanctification, but this next one does: "But little children are holy, being *sanctified through the atonement* of Jesus Christ; and this is what the scriptures mean" (D&C 74:7). It would appear that Christ's Atonement, His "preparatory redemption," applied through faith in His

---

127 *Hymns*, no. 189.

name in the premortal existence, had power to justify and sanctify us in the first estate. Once again, Alma confirmed this notion. Speaking of the premortal existence, he said: "Therefore they were . . . *sanctified,* and their garments were washed white through the blood of the Lamb. Now they, after being *sanctified* by the Holy Ghost, having their garments made white, being pure and spotless before God, *could not look upon sin save it were with abhorrence*; and there were many, exceedingly great many, who were made *pure.*"[128]

Sanctification entails spiritual progression, and, obviously, we progressed before we came to mortality. However, it appears that the sanctification we can achieve in this life is greater (or perhaps different) due to the fact that we have a body and can learn and grow so much more. We know that all who come to earth were pardoned and declared innocent, but some moved farther along the path than others. "Having their agency," Elder McConkie said, "all the spirits of men, while yet in the Eternal Presence, developed aptitudes, talents, capacities, and abilities of every sort, kind, and degree. During the long expanse of life which then was, an infinite variety of talents and abilities came into being. As the ages rolled, no two spirits remained alike. . . . The whole house of Israel . . . was inclined toward spiritual things."[129] Similarly, Joseph Fielding Smith taught, "The spirits of men were not equal. They may have had an equal start, and we know they were all innocent in the beginning; but the right of free agency which was given to them enabled some to outstrip others and thus, through the eons of immortal existence, to become more intelligent, more faithful, for they were free to act for themselves, to think for themselves,

---

128   Alma 13:11–12; emphasis added; A close reading of the context of Alma 13:1–12 will bear out the point that all these things are occurring in the premortal existence.

129   *The Mortal Messiah: From Bethlehem to Calvary,* 4 vols. (Salt Lake City: Deseret Book, 1979), 1:23.

to receive the truth or rebel against it."[130] Sanctification was apparently in operation to the point that various individuals were able to attain to a great status, as is evidenced in Abraham 3, with the many "noble and great ones." Jehovah, the premortal Christ, was even able to become "a god before he came into the world," Lorenzo Snow said, "and yet his knowledge was taken from him. He did not know his former greatness, neither do we know what greatness we had attained to before we came here, but he had to pass through an ordeal, as we have to, without knowing or realizing at the time the greatness and importance of his mission and works."[131]

All of this leads to an interesting yet tangential question: If there were faith in Christ and repentance of sin in the premortal existence and the Holy Ghost was operational (see Alma 13:1–15), were there ordinances as well? Joseph Fielding Smith taught that "during the ages in which we dwelt in the premortal state we not only developed our various characteristics and showed our worthiness and ability, or the lack of it, but we were also where such progress could be observed. . . . There was a Church organization there. The heavenly beings were living in a perfectly arranged society. Every person knew his place. Priesthood . . . had been conferred and the leaders were chosen to officiate. *Ordinances pertaining to that pre-existence were required* and the love of God prevailed."[132]

As Latter-day Saints, we do not believe in certain commonly taught Christian doctrines, such as original sin, the total depravity of man, infant baptism, and predestination to grace. These doctrines are interrelated but are nonetheless false since they begin with the wrong antecedent—mainly, a misunderstanding

---

130 *Doctrines of Salvation,* 1:59.

131 Quoted in Wendy L. Watson, "Change—It's Always a Possibility!" 7 April 1998 in *BYU Speeches,* http://speeches.byu.edu/reader/reader.php?id=2159.

132 *Way to Perfection* (Salt Lake City: Deseret Book, 1949), 51; emphasis added.

of the Atonement in the premortal existence. It could be argued that the true doctrine is indeed one of the core and pivotal doctrines of the Restoration. It breathes life into so many of our other doctrines, clarifying and binding them closely together in a perfect and complete whole.

As we come to understand the premortal nature of the Atonement, we also are given insight into the true nature of Satan's rebellion in that premortal sphere—that is to say, he and his followers (the third part) didn't just reject God's plan, they apparently made the choice not to accept the power of the Atonement in the first estate. Thus, they were disqualified to come to mortality to gain a physical body. This denial of the Atonement is what constitutes the "unpardonable sin," whether committed in the premortal existence or here in mortality—not just in belief but, more importantly, in application. All who come to earth will eventually be redeemed to a kingdom of glory (that is to say, they are all saved by the Atonement) except sons of perdition since they choose not to be saved (see D&C 76:43). Perhaps this is why those sons of perdition who did receive bodies are so much worse off—they applied the Atonement once but not here in mortality. Thus says the revelation, "It had been better for them never to have been born" (D&C 76:32).

We developed talents in the premortal realm, one of which was the talent of spirituality, including the ability to have faith, repent, and apply the infinite Atonement. What a comforting and powerful doctrine for individuals who sometimes wonder whether or not they can fully repent in this life, whether or not they can access the Atonement and truly become clean. Because of the knowledge we are blessed with in the Book of Mormon and from other modern-day scriptures concerning this doctrine, we can be reassured it's possible because it's happened for us once before.

Three Pillars of Existence and Eternity: The Chiastic and Doctrinal Elegance of 2 Nephi 2

God is giving away the spiritual secrets of the universe, but are we listening?
—*Elder Neal A. Maxwell*[133]

Treasure these things up in your hearts, and let the solemnities of eternity rest upon your minds.
—*D&C 43:34*

THUS FAR WE'VE COVERED A number of topics in relation to God's time and our time in this mortal probation. In this last chapter we will examine the three pillars of eternity and existence—the Creation, the Fall, and the Atonement—and how God's prophets, particularly in the Book of Mormon, intentionally used a beautiful, powerful, enlightening style of writing to reinforce the doctrine that His work is, indeed, one eternal round. The concepts of existence and eternity are deep in their doctrinal and philosophical ramifications. There is so little we understand and

---

133 "Our Creator's Cosmos," Brigham Young University August 13, 2002.

so much that is yet to be revealed. Paul reminds us: "While we look not at the things which are seen, but at the things which are not seen: for the things which are seen are temporal; but the things which are not seen are eternal" (2 Corinthians 4:18). When it comes to the hard doctrines, to the pearls of greatest price, the God of heaven often resorts to parables and symbols to teach us, as well as esoteric imagery and veiled phrases.

Christ's disciples asked, "Why speakest thou . . . in parables? He answered and said unto them, Because *it is given unto you to know the mysteries of the kingdom of heaven, but to them it is not given.* For whosoever hath, to him shall be given, and he shall have more abundance: but whosoever hath not, from him shall be taken away even that he hath. Therefore speak I to them in parables: because they seeing see not; and hearing they hear not, neither do they understand" (Matthew 13:10–13; emphasis added).

Parables and symbols thus reveal God's word, but they also conceal it as well. God imparts His word to those who are willing to ask and knock. He unlocks the door of wisdom to those who seek diligently, with real intent. Thus we see that "it is given unto many to know the mysteries of God; nevertheless they are laid under a strict command that they shall not impart only according to the portion of his word which he doth grant unto the children of men, *according to the heed and diligence* which they give unto him. And therefore, he that will harden his heart, *the same receiveth the lesser portion* of the word; and he that will not harden his heart, *to him is given the greater portion* of the word, until it is given unto him to know the mysteries of God until he know them in full" (Alma 12:9–10).

The central and vital doctrines of the gospel are also revealed in highly structured word play and carefully coded discourses. The primary purpose of this chapter is to examine the doctrinal concepts of existence and eternity by analyzing a unique chiastic structure in 2 Nephi 2, which consists of Lehi's counsel to his son

Jacob.[134] Our hope is to be able to see the place and importance of the doctrines of the Fall and the Atonement and how it is that these two core doctrines help define, relate to, and give meaning to our existence and provide a framework through which we can better understand the concept and reality of the great expanse of eternity and how all things are truly before God at all times. Furthermore, by using assessment criteria proposed by John Welch to measure and ascertain the authenticity of potential chiastic structures, we will attempt to determine the strength and potential validity of this "Lehi" chiasmus.[135]

We'll also take a look at several other chiastic structures in the Book of Mormon (2 Nephi 1–4) that are closely related to the proposed structure. Their inclusion will help establish one particular facet of the assessment criteria. As far as I can determine, these other structures, as well as the one proposed

---

134 "Chiasmus is a style of writing known in antiquity and mused by many ancient and some modern writers. It consists of arranging a series of words or ideas in one order, and then repeating it in reverse order. In the hands of a skillful writer, this literary form can serve several purposes. The repeating of key words in the two halves underlines the importance of the concepts they present. Furthermore, the main idea of the passage is placed at the turning point where the second half begins, which emphasizes it. The repeating form also enhances clarity and speeds memorizing. Readers (or listeners) gain a pleasing sense of completeness as the passage returns at the end to the idea that began it. Identifying the presence of chiasmus in a composition can reveal many complex and subtle features of the text." (John Welch, "A Masterpiece: Alma 36," in *Rediscovering the Book of Mormon*, Provo, Utah: Maxwell Institute)

135 See John W. Welch, "Criteria for Identifying and Evaluating the presence of Chiasmus," *Journal of Book of Mormon Studies*, April 2, 1995.

in 2 Nephi 2, have never been previously assessed.[136]

Over the past several decades, many examples of chiastic structure in the Book of Mormon have been proffered. Over forty years ago John Welch noted that the presence of chiasmus is important as it may serve as a strong indication of the Book of Mormon's ancient and artistic composition.[137] John Welch has stated:

> Not all chiasms, however, are created equal. They differ in purpose, precision, and artistic achievement. Some are very clear; others are not. Some are very long; others are short. We must learn to look carefully to know whether a passage may be an actual chiasm and whether it is significant. After evaluating hundreds of proposed chiasms in a wide variety of lengthy texts, I have found that only a few texts unmistakably rate as planned, successful chiasms. Alma 36 is one of the best. Alma 36 was one of the first chiasms I discovered within the Book of Mormon in 1967. Many years later, it still remains one of my favorites. It is a masterpiece of composition, as good as any other use of chiasmus in world literature, and it deserves wide recognition and appreciation. I cannot imagine that its complex and purposeful structure happened unintentionally. Its sophistication as a

---

136 The Lehi chiasmus in 2 Nephi 2 is a structure that I first encountered several years ago while doing doctoral work at Purdue University. I was excited and thrilled with the thought that the possibility of chiasmus existed. Accordingly I wrote to John Welch at BYU to seek his opinion. He was kind enough to send me his Chiasmus Bibliography along with the criteria for assessing its presence. Due to work, school, and other life issues, I did not pursue the project at that time, but I continued to ponder it over the years and have recently come back to it and made some additional and amazing discoveries.

137 John A. Tvedtnes, Insights, the newsletter by FARMS, Feb. 1999.

piece of literature definitely shows Alma's skill as a writer.[138]

The same thing can be said of Lehi's chiasmus in 2 Nephi 2. Like Welch's chiasm in Alma 36, the Lehi chiasm in 2 Nephi 2 has a high degree of soteriology, that is to say, both chiasms have as their central focus the core doctrines of the gospel, especially as it relates to salvation. I believe that Lehi's chiasmus in 2 Nephi 2 is thus a firm and profound buttress to Alma's chiasmus in Alma 36: it shows that such complex, doctrinal, and lengthy chiasmus is less likely to be coincidental.

Where the central purpose of the Book of Mormon is to testify of Christ,[139] it would be of interest to ascertain whether or not chiastic structures in the Book of Mormon tend to focus on core doctrines of the gospel like the Creation, the Fall, and the Atonement—the three "preeminent" doctrines that Elder McConkie refers to as the three pillars of eternity.[140] I would add, as we shall attempt to show in the examples that follow, that these three core doctrines are also the three pillars of *existence*. But first let's look at an analysis of the chiastic structure of 2 Nephi 2:

---

138 John Welch, "A Masterpiece: Alma 36" in *Rediscovering the Book of Mormon*, 116.

139 Title Page of the Book of Mormon; also see 1 Nephi 6:4

140 Bruce R. McConkie, Devotional address given at Brigham Young University on 17 February 1981

A Jacob, <u>I speak unto you</u>; Thou art my first born <u>in the days of my tribulation</u> (v.1)

 B thou art redeemed because of the righteousness of thy Redeemer: he cometh to <u>bring salvation</u> unto men (v.3)

  C He shall <u>minister in the flesh</u> (v.4)

   D For the <u>spirit is the same</u> (v.4)

    E <u>the way is prepared</u> from the fall of man (v.4)

    F and <u>salvation is free</u> (v.4)

     G instructed sufficiently that they <u>know good from evil</u>. By the <u>law they are cut off</u> (v.5)

      H <u>redemption</u> cometh

       I in and through the Holy <u>Messiah</u> (v.6)

      J The Atonement (vv. 6–10) Christ's atonement makes possible eternal life—spiritual rebirth

  J1 he is full of grace and truth. . . . offereth himself . . . to answer the ends of the law (v.6-7)

  J2 no flesh that can dwell in the presence of God (v.8)

  J3 resurrection of the dead, being the first that should rise (v.8)

   J4 he shall make intercession for all the children of men (v.9)

   J5 they that believe in him, shall be saved (v.9)

  J4' because of the intercession for all (v.10)

  J3' all men cometh unto God

 J2' they stand in the presence of Him (v.10)

J1' the truth and holiness which is in him. Wherefore, the ends of the law (v.10)

 K there is an opposition [with sweet and bitter examples] (v.11)

  L must needs have been (v.12)

  M created for a thing of naught (v.12)

   N the end of its creation (v.12)

    O the wisdom of God, and his eternal purposes (v.12)

     P1 if there is no God, we are not, neither the earth:

     P2 for there could have been no creation of things

P3 neither to act

P4 nor to be acted upon (v.13)

  Q wherefore, all things must have vanished away (v.13)

P1' there is a God

P2' and he hath created all things

P3' both things to act,

P4' and things to be acted upon (v.14)

  O' to bring about his eternal purposes (v,15)

    N' in the end of man, after that he created our first parents (v.15)

      M' all things which are created (v.15)

      L' it must needs be (v.15)

    K' there was an opposition / [with sweet and bitter fruits] (v.15)

J6 an angel of God . . . had fallen . . . wherefore he became a devil (v.17)

 J7 knowing good and evil (v.18)

  J8 after Adam and Eve had partaken . . . they were driven out of the Garden of Eden (v.19)

    J9 the family of all the earth (v.20)

      J10 the children of men

        J11 days . . . were prolonged, according to the will of God (v.21)

          J12 that they might repent while in the flesh (v.21)

        J11' their time was lengthened, according to the commandments which the Lord God gave (v.21)

      J10' the children of men (v.21)

    J9' all men . . . were lost (v.21)

  J8' if Adam had not transgressed . . . he would have remained in the Garden of Eden (v.22

 J7' doing no good, for they knew no sin (v.23)

J6' Adam fell that men might be . . . men are that they might have joy (v.25)

    J' The Fall (18-25) Adam fall makes mortality possible—physical birth

      I' Messiah cometh in the fulness of time,

H' that he might <u>redeem</u> the children of men from the fall (v.26)

G' they are free forever <u>knowing good from evil</u>; . . . save it be by <u>the punishment of law</u> (v.26)

F' Wherefore, <u>men are free</u> according to the flesh;

E' <u>all things are given them which are expedient unto man</u> (v.27)

D' the will of <u>his Holy Spirit</u> (v.28)

C' according to the <u>will of the flesh</u> (v.29)

B' which giveth the spirit of the Devil power to captivate, to <u>bring you down to hell</u> (v.29)

A' I <u>have spoken these few words unto you all</u>, my sons, <u>in the last days of my probation</u> (v.30)

Lehi's chiasmus in 2 Nephi 2 is not only protracted in length, but it is doctrinally complex, literarily rich, and eloquently elegant. In fact, there may be no other chiasm like this in all of scripture. This chiasm contains within its structure two profoundly significant yet smaller doctrinal chiasms. These two smaller chiasms, as will be seen, are neither random nor coincidental but have strong doctrinal connections and ramifications that would immeasurably strengthen the case for intentional chiastic structure in Lehi's counsel to his son Jacob.[141]

Criteria for Identifying and Evaluating the Presence of Chiasmus

John Welch has determined "fifteen criteria one can use to measure the strength or weakness of a proposed chiastic pattern in a given text. The need for rigor in such studies depends primarily on how the results of the proposed structural analyses will be used. Ultimately, analysts may not know with certainty whether an author created inverted parallel structures intentionally or not; but by examining a text from various angles, one may assess the likelihood that an author consciously employed chiasmus to achieve specific literary purposes."[142] Welch suggests that "some texts are strongly and precisely chiastic, while in other cases it

---

141 At first I was somewhat surprised with what I had noticed. I must admit that although I found my own analysis to be in many ways creative, I felt at the same time that it was so unusual that I wondered whether or not the chiastic structure would be viewed as self-evident to others as it was to me. I doubted my own views sufficiently to seek perspectives from other broadly informed readers and even a few who have worked in the area of chiastic analysis. Even before considering the possibility of publication, at least eight individuals were consulted. At first I suspected that very few would come up with an outline or a chiastic arrangement anything similar to mine. To my surprise, most, if not all, where extremely intrigued and could see the same structure I was seeing. One individual well versed in chiastic analysis told me he was "stunned" at the structure of 2 Nephi 2 and was baffled that he had not seen this before. Two individuals who did preliminary peer reviews indicated that they were impressed and could see in a self-evident way the structure and even encouraged me to take it into more formal publication arenas. One highly noted expert in the field even commented in a written correspondence to me, "I do believe that this is one of the most extensive efforts so far to try to work through this text in this way." Suffice it to say, enough people, in my opinion, have reworked the chiastic approach to 2 Nephi 2 enough times, coming up essentially with the same chiastic configuration as myself and others, that I am sufficiently persuaded that a macro chiasm is indeed to be objectively found in this profoundly doctrinal and rhetorically powerful chapter.

142 Welch, Chiasmus Bibliography.

may only be possible to speak of a general presence of balance or framing."[143]

Admittedly, my analysis relies almost slavishly on Welch's assessment criteria so that I might provide a simple and straightforward methodological framework that adds objectivity and rigor to the analysis. However, it should be noted that there are several articles dealing with criteria for identifying chiasmus.[144] An analysis such as this one on 2 Nephi 2, which depends extensively on satisfying a particular criteria, would do well to utilize the full range of criteria, in order to have a more broadly based analysis. However, after thorough examination, it is my opinion that these other frameworks are so sufficiently considered and inherently included in Welch's criteria that I am not persuaded that I or anyone would come up with any different conclusion by utilizing other methodological approaches. Moreover, rigid rules do not tell the whole story of chiastic analysis. Overall sensitivity and "aesthetics," as well as common sense also play an important role in the analysis of such a complex scripture block.

So let's make an analysis of the proposed chiasmus in 2 Nephi 2. The elements that follow in bold and italics will contain Welch's criteria, followed by the assessment of the Lehi chiasm.

Objectivity

To what degree is the proposed pattern clearly evident in the text? If the process of identifying chiasmus is to produce verifiable results, the inverted parallel orders must be objectively evident. If a proposed chiasm consists of elements that are objectively observable in the text, rather than depending on distant parallels or clever linkages that require imaginative commentary to explain, it is more likely that the

---

143 Welch, Chiasmus Bibliography.

144 Nils Lund, Chiasmus in the New Testament (1942); Craig Blomberg, "The Structure of 2 Corinthians," Criswell Theological Review 4 (1989):3-20; M. J. Boda, "Chiasmus in Ubiquity: Symmetrical Mirages in Nehemiah. 9,"Journal for the Study of the Old Testament, 1996, 21:55-70; Boyd F. Edwards and W. Farrell Edwards, "Does Chiasmus Appear in the Book of Mormon by Chance?" (2004); Paul Gaechter, *Die literarische Kunst im Matthäus-Evangelium* (The Literary Art in the Gospel of Matthew) (1965).

chiastic character of the text is strong and less likely that the reader has imposed an arrangement upon the text which he or she alone has brought to it. The more evident an arrangement, the greater the degree of chiasticity.

The main elements in Lehi's chiasmus (2 Nephi 2) are indeed objectively observable; more than forty pairs of key words or phrases, both synonymous and antithetical, are identical or nearly identical. No distant parallels, clever linkages, or imaginative commentary are needed in order to see the structure that exists in Lehi's words to his son Jacob.

The first element of the structure not only demonstrates this point, but it is apparently a skillful and intriguing device employed by Father Lehi in teaching his sons—"And now, Jacob, *I speak unto you*" (v. 1; emphasis added)—when paired with the end of his counsel, which also forms the end of chapter 2: "*I have spoken these few words unto you all*, my sons" (v. 30; emphasis added). Why intriguing? Considering the fact that Lehi is giving counsel to all of his sons in what appears to be a group gathering (2 Nephi 1–3); and considering the fact that he probably wants to teach all of them the vital doctrines of the Creation, the Fall, and the Atonement as found in 2 Nephi 2, it is not difficult to conceive that Lehi, so as not to bore, alienate, or be thought of as "preachy" by his wicked sons, directs his comments to Jacob, knowing that the rest would probably listen and in the process be touched (hopefully) by the Spirit. After first directing his remarks to Jacob, he concludes by telling his sons that he has spoken to all of them (see v. 30). Furthermore, this switch from the singular "you" to the plural "you all" is not uncommon. The concept of speaking rhetorically in the singular for the benefit of the larger group is not only evident herein but characteristic of Hebraic writing, from which the Book of Mormon claims its linguistic origins.[145]

These chiastic elements in the introductory and concluding phrases also bear another interesting similarity. The words

145 See Kevin L. Barney, "Enallage in the Book of Mormon," *Journal of Book of Mormon Studies*, 3/1 [1994]: 113–47.

"Now, Jacob, I speak unto you: Thou art my first-born *in the days of my tribulation in the wilderness*" (2 Nephi 2:1) compares remarkably well with "I have spoken these few words unto you all, my sons, *in the last days of my probation*" (2 Nephi 2:30). In fact, these main corresponding phrases contain five direct elements either in word or phrase: I/I; speak/spoken; unto you/unto you all; Jacob/sons; days/days; my tribulation/my probation.

This occurrence of matching phrases (not just single words), often known as parallel phrases or parallel lines, can be found in other paired elements throughout the scripture block. This is significant because we are dealing with a translation from an ancient language into English. In fact, parallel lines or phrases may be more important here than parallel words, for words can vary across translations, but phrases or concepts show much more evidence of intended purpose, especially in this case, where there is a strong doctrinal chiasmus. Such use of parallel lines and phrases is characteristic of Hebraic poetry.[146]

Other such examples of objective elements that need no stretching to be considered chiastic include: "Wherefore, *redemption* cometh in and through the *Holy Messiah*" (v. 6; emphasis added) and its counterpart, "the *Messiah* cometh in the fulness of time, that he may *redeem* the children of men" (v. 26; emphasis added). Here we see the nominal form paired with its verbal cognate. Most of the elements in this chiasm are directly related in word as can be seen in the preceding structural chart. Notice the midpoint of the Fall and the Atonement chiasms: "that they might repent while in the flesh (v. 21)" and "they that believe in him, shall be saved (v.9)" The association is clear.

Though the phrases labeled B/B' share no direct words (other than "bring"), I would argue there is still a clear antithetical correlation among three corresponding elements: "thou art

---

146 See Kevin L. Barney, "Poetic Diction and Parallel Word Pairs in the Book of Mormon," *Journal of Book of Mormon Studies*, 4/2 [1995]: 15–81.

redeemed because of the righteousness of thy Redeemer: he cometh to bring salvation unto men" (v. 3) and "which giveth the spirit of the Devil power to captivate, to bring you down to hell" (v. 29). Notice the correlation between the themes of action, facilitator, and result:

1. Action: "redeemed"   vs.   "captivate"
2. Facilitator: "Redeemer"   vs.   "Devil"
3. Result: "bring salvation" vs. "bring you down to hell"

Illustratively, a nearly perfect, similar example (in form and content) of extended antithetical parallelism of Alma 9:28 has been discussed by Donald W. Parry.[147] For purposes of comparison I will outline his analysis using the "action/result/facilitator" paradigm employed above: "Therefore, prepare ye the way of the Lord, for the time is at hand that all men shall reap a reward of their works, according to that which they have been—*if they have been righteous they shall reap the salvation of their souls, according to the power and deliverance of Jesus Christ; and if they have been evil they shall reap the damnation of their souls, according to the power and captivation of the devil."*

1. Action: "If they have been righteous"
2. Result: "they shall reap the salvation of their souls,"
3. Facilitator: "according to the power and deliverance of Jesus Christ"

Parry compares this to the latter part of the verse, which states:

1. Action: "and if they have been evil"
2. Result: "they shall reap the damnation of their souls"
3. Facilitator: "according to the power and captivation of the devil"

---

147 Parry, Donald W., "Antithetical Parallelism in the Book of Mormon," Provo, Utah: Maxwell Institute, Chapter 47

Parry notes, "In the first strophe the words "righteous," "salvation," "deliverance," and "Jesus Christ" stand in direct contrast to the terms of the second strophe—"evil," "damnation," "captivation," and "devil." Both strophes begin with an "if" statement immediately followed by the results that come from righteousness or evil. The sides are clearly drawn between good and evil."

A further example and illustration of antithetical parallelism in the Lehi chiasm can be found with the J6/J6' pair (see verse 17 and verse 25):

1. Facilitator: "an angel of god"
2. Action: "had fallen"
3. Result: "wherefore he became a devil"

   Compare with

1. Facilitator: "Adam"
2. Action: "fell"
3. Result: "that men might be . . . that they might have joy"

It is interesting to note that both these individuals "fell" but that the end results were diametrically opposite, one being a bitter outcome (the devil), the other sweet (Adam and humankind's existence). The doctrinal and philosophical ramifications are interesting here, given human nature and potential, not to mention God's will in letting us experience opposition. This is to say that tribulation (opposition) can be either a blessing or a curse. The P/P' pair also is interesting in this regard, as the reader will note, especially given the fact that it is at the center of the chiasm.

Finally, consider the J8/J8' pair (see verses 19 and 22):

1. Facilitator: Adam and Eve
2. Action: had partaken
3. Result: they were driven out of the Garden of Eden

Compare with

1. Facilitator: Adam
2. Action: if [he] had not transgressed
3. Result: he would have remained in the Garden of Eden

Parry surmises that "antithetical parallelism not only contrasts two ideas, but also connects them. The meaning of the contrasted items separates them clearly, but the parallelistic format joins them so that the reader must consider them together. One purpose of this poetic form is thus to allow, or even force, the reader to make a mental comparison, and often a choice, between two diametrically opposed but related ideas. Whether consciously or intuitively, the reader sees in antithetical parallelism a unique reciprocity, as well as a strong contrast between the two elements."

Parry concludes, "Antithetical parallelism has the ability to produce an emotional response in the original audience and also in subsequent readers that leads them to follow the teachings. Comparison between two terms has always been an accepted tool of rhetoricians to invoke the reader's involvement. . . . Recognizing this antithetical parallel structure can help us see more clearly the issues that writers of the Book of Mormon wanted us to focus on. Appreciating the connections and contrasts between the ideas that they felt were most important may lead us to feel as they felt and act as they admonish us to act."[148]

Interestingly, there are additional instances of juxtaposed, chiastically corresponding, antithetically parallel phrases which lend weight to this argument throughout Lehi's chiasm. This is not only intriguing but somewhat expected since the whole center point of the Lehi chiasm (discussed later) focuses on "opposition" in all things. It seems an appropriate form given the content. Furthermore, Lehi frequently and artistically

---

148 Parry, Donald W., "Antithetical Parallelism in the Book of Mormon," Provo, Utah: Maxwell Institute, Chapter 47

makes use of synonymous parallelism, antithetical parallelism, and synthetic parallelism, all of which are characteristic of Hebrew poetry. The balance among the three types is equal— nine pairs of each of these three types— throughout the entire 2 Nephi 2 chiasm.[149]

Purpose

Is there an identifiable literary reason why the author might have employed chiasmus in this text? Chiasmus is useful for several purposes, such as concentrating attention on the main point of a passage by placing it at the central turning point, drawing meaningful contrasts, aiding in memorization, or emphasizing the feeling of closure upon the conclusion of a lengthy repetition.

There is indeed an identifiable literary reason why Lehi may have imposed chiasmus on his words in 2 Nephi 2. The central chiasm within the chiasm begins and ends with "opposition in all things." In this case the chiastic structure frames a meaningful and well-balanced contrast of the interrelated doctrines of the Fall and the Atonement. Christ suffers physical death to make possible spiritual life; Adam suffers spiritual death to initiate mortal life, that is, the Fall and the Atonement are paralleled. When the middle of the chiasm is examined, Elder McConkie's third pillar of eternity, the Creation appears encased in the Fall/atonement parallel. It is interesting that the Creation is the

---

149 In synonymous parallelism, the idea of the second line is a restatement of the idea of the first line (see Proverbs 18:7). In antithetical parallelism, the idea of the second line is the opposite of the idea in the first line (see Proverbs 18:23). In synthetic parallelism, which is not really parallelism at all, related thoughts are brought together to emphasize similarities, contrasts, or other correlations. Lehi uses all three types throughout this chapter.

doctrine that rests at the center point.[150]

It would appear hardly a coincidence that Lehi, as a prophet who "was learned in all language," would resort to such form and style in transmitting these core and fundamental doctrines not only to his sons but also to future readers of the Book of Mormon. It would appear that chiasmus in the Book of Mormon, especially if intentional on part of Book of Mormon authors, is much more likely to be found in passages where there is a clear and purposeful relationship between form and content; such as in the case of 2 Nephi 2, between the description of how the world and existence came into being (along with the counterbalancing realities of the Fall and the Atonement) and the literary structure of those descriptions. Furthermore, the use of chiastic structure in this profoundly doctrinal and philosophical scripture block enables the prophet Lehi to dwell upon his multifaceted themes with an almost inexhaustible variety of expression and coloring. Indeed, Lehi's words in 2 Nephi 2 demand our attention.

Boundaries

A chiasm is stronger if it operates across a literary unit as a whole and not only upon fragments or sections which overlap or cut across significant organizational lines intrinsic to the text. To the extent that the proposed structure crosses over natural barriers, unnaturally

150 Some scholars today point out the fact that the Rabbis of the Mishnah considered the Creation narrative to be one of the most esoteric of all texts (see Moshe Klinean, Introduction to the Structured Mishnah, An Address to the Talmud Faculty of the Jewish Theological Seminary of America, March 21, 2005). The theological concepts of creation and the reality of existence (the exact midpoint, in fact, of the Lehi chiasm!) were theological verities transmitted not only by allegory but by carefully crafted and styled writing, thus insuring that multiple forms would protect and carry forward through generations the written record along with its deeper meaning. Exegesis (or interpretation) of such theologically intense texts thus would require the learner to deconstruct the passage into an almost visual pattern or map in order to more fully grasp the doctrinal message.

chops sentences in half, or falls short of discernible boundaries in the text as a whole, the more dubious the suggested chiasm becomes.

This chiasm clearly operates across a distinct literary unit; in this case, Lehi's counsel to his son Jacob. The boundaries here are distinct and precise from the very beginning in verse 1 to the very end of the chapter, which is also the natural beginning and ending point of Lehi's counsel to Jacob and his other sons. According to John Welch, "Whenever one reads a text, especially a text with ancient origins, one ought to be mindful of the text's division into segments or units, and that chiasmus afforded a seriously needed element of internal organization in ancient writing."[151] It should be noted that 2 Nephi 2, as it stands in current editions of the scriptures, was actually part of chapter 1 in the original 1830 edition of the Book of Mormon. However, regardless of the edition or version being examined—whether the current edition, 1830 edition, 1830 printer's manuscript, or Royal Skousen's treatment of "sense-lines" in *The Book of Mormon: The Earliest Text*—the structure remains the same as it comprises a self-contained literary unit. This marking and framing done by father Lehi is clearly evident not only in his counsel to Jacob as found in 2 Nephi 2, but, as we shall see, it is evident in Lehi's counsel to his others sons and daughters as well.

Although I have chosen as the midpoint of the chiasm—the phrase "all things must have vanished away"—it may well be that included in this midpoint is the next phrase: "And now my sons, I speak unto you these things for your profit and learning." Thus the chiasm has as its beginning, middle, and end essentially the same idea:

---

151   John W. Welch, "What Does Chiasmus in the Book of Mormon Prove?" in *Book of Mormon Authorship Revisited: The Evidence for Ancient Origins*, ed. Noel B. Reynolds (Provo, Utah: FARMS, 1997), 205. Welch also writes that "the design and depth of the Book of Mormon often comes to light only when the book is studied with chiastic and other ancient literary principles in mind." Ibid., 222.

- And now, Jacob, I speak unto you . . . (v. 1)
- And now, my sons, I speak unto you . . . (v. 13)
- I have spoken these few words unto you all,
my sons (v. 30)

With this being the case, the chiasm is extremely well balanced and has logical boundaries. In fact, this idea is supported by the fact that there are only three times such a phrase is used. It's unlikely to be coincidental. Now, one could conclude that there is a shift in audience in the middle of 2 Nephi 2 from just Jacob to all of Lehi's sons, and, therefore a shift in topic. However, that is an untenable conclusion since, as can be seen, Lehi uses this pivot point to reverse his logic from negative conclusions about God, creation, and agency to a positive position about the exact same elements. It is clearly the same literary unit. That the shift in the middle away from "Jacob" to "all the sons" conforms to the use of the antithetical is compelling. Welch has recognized a particularly interesting point of criteria in this regard from Nils Lund, who has noted that "at the center there is often a change in the trend of thought, and an antithetic idea is introduced"[152]—precisely what occurs at the midpoint of Lehi's chiasm.

As mentioned earlier, it almost seems as though Lehi starts by giving counsel to Jacob with the intent of having the others listen in, and then, midway through his doctrinal discourse, he brings them all in. The rhetoric, the content, and the form all mesh together. Is it possible the midpoint "I speak unto you these things for your *profit* and *learning*" is more than a redundancy? Perhaps the doctrinal part of instruction is for their "profit" and the aesthetic part is for their "learning." Lehi is meeting both objectives.

I am persuaded, though, that the phrase "all things would vanish away" would still be part of the midpoint (maybe it's

---

152 *Chiasmus in the New Testament* [1942]; see http://chiasmusresources. johnwwelchresources.com/criteria-chart.

both), and a significant one, because of the existential flavor of the argument Lehi is making: You need opposites, including the Fall and the Atonement. If you don't have opposition, you don't have existence. William Blake in "The Marriage of Heaven and Hell," makes the assertion that opposites, such as attraction and repulsion, reason and energy, love and hate, are necessary to human existence. In "The Paradox of Existence: Philosophy and Aesthetics in the Young Schelling," Leonardo V. Distaso observes that existence is a function of opposition and that existence is possible only if there is opposition. He states also (commenting on the opposite pairs in 2 Nephi 2): "When we stand back and observe these sets of opposites as a group, we notice that they form the purposive structure of human existence, and its total negation, which underlie the gospel in all its aspects. Within this structure all humankind collectively and individually face the grand possibilities of their existence, that is, they face life and death, happiness and misery, as the caretakers of their own lives."[153] He continues, "There indeed 'must needs be an opposition in all things.' For if there were not, if the fundamental opposition of life and death with its numerous degrees did not exist, then all modes of existence in time and eternity would not be possible. God himself would not be and all created things would vanish away."[154]

Competition with Other Forms

Chiasmus is more dominant in a passage when it is the only structuring device employed there. Chiasmus becomes less significant to the extent that a competing literary device or explanation of the arrangement of the words or thoughts more readily accounts for an apparently chiastic placement of elements.

---

153   A. D. Sorensen, "Lehi on God's Law and an Opposition in All Things," in *Second Nephi, The Doctrinal Structure*, ed. Monte S. Nyman and Charles D. Tate Jr. (Provo, UT: Religious Studies Center, Brigham Young University, 1989), 107–32

154   Ibid.

It is evident that chiasmus is the only structural device employed in 2 Nephi 2. There are no other literary forms or styles that account for the arrangement of the words and thoughts in this text. It is, in fact, simply remarkable how well this particular literary unit functions and lends itself to the chiastic form. There are instances, to be sure, where the literary use of opposites is employed, but such use is not a separate form but an interesting illustration of the main form. In other words, Lehi uses opposites, but his purpose is to illustrate the chiastic element of opposition in all things.

For example, the overall structure seems, on the surface, to omit a significant passage in verse 11: "If not so, my first-born in the wilderness, righteousness could not be brought to pass, neither wickedness, neither holiness nor misery, neither good nor bad. Wherefore, all things must needs be a compound in one; wherefore, if it should be one body it must needs remain as dead, having no life neither death, nor corruption nor incorruption, happiness nor misery, neither sense nor insensibility." However, all this falls under the opposition-in-all-things element as an illustration, thus potentially not part of the structure. It is akin to a parenthetical statement. Additionally, it should be noted that as a single structure it does have a poetic nature to it.

Verse 15 has a similar parenthetical statement as well, in that it simply describes the sweet and bitter. And, like verse 11, it is preceded by the phrase "opposition in all things." Thus one paired (and parenthetical) chiasm mentions the "bitter and sweet" while the other lists them out. Verse 13 is missing a significant line, but it too highlights the necessity of the sweet and the bitter. And, although the beginning element is more complete as opposed to the latter element, which is simply a summary, it is an exact extension of those last three items.

Length

The longer the proposed chiasm, the higher its degree of chiasticity. In other words, a chiasm composed of six words introduced in one order and then repeated in the opposite order is more extensively chiastic than a structure composed of three repeated words. Having a large number of proposed elements, however, is not alone very significant, for all the elements must bear their own weight. An extended chiasm is probably not much stronger than its weakest links.

The chiasmus in 2 Nephi 2 is definitely long, with over forty distinct elements, each with vivid and compelling purpose. Furthermore, most elements do not just comprise one word but almost always contain phrases with multiple identical words. Not only are there no weak links, but each element also bears significant doctrinal weight that contributes to the overall message of the text.

Density

How many words are there between the dominant elements? The more compact the proposed structure, or the fewer irrelevancies between its elements, the higher the degree of chiasticity. Tightness in the text is indicative of greater craftsmanship, rigor, focus, intention, and clarity. In assessing the density of a passage, all significant words and phrases appearing in the system must be considered. What is disregarded or omitted is often just as important as what is included. Thus, if a proposed chiasm involves only a few terms spread out over a long text, it has a low density.

The structure is definitely compact. Almost every verse contributes a key element. It is not simply a few words or phrases parsed out over a long text. In fact, Lehi's use of chiasmus becomes even more significant because of the *doctrinal* density involved. Nearly every verse makes a significant contribution. The chiasm is tight, both literarily and doctrinally, and rarely disregards any significant words or phrases. By comparison, Alma's chiasm (Alma 36), which has excellent density, has 17 pairs of chiastic corresponding elements spread over 30 verses, or a density of 1.13 elements per verse; while Lehi's chiasm (2 Nephi 2) has over 40 pairs spread over 30 verses with 3 nonpaired chiastic centers (one for each of the three chiasms in the structure), for a total of over 80 significant chiastic elements, or a density of 2.67 elements per verse, making its density greater (117 percent more) than even Alma's chiasm. Given as a whole, this chiastic structure is systematic and focused, with an undeniably clear sense of intention.

To be fair, there are some gaps with important words and phrases not unaccounted for in my proposed structure. Despite the "cheerleading" (as some might call it) that might be inherent in parts of my analysis, it is my hope to be as rigorous and self-critical as necessary in order to substantiate the claims I'm attempting to lay out. One weakness for which I do not have an answer is a glaring gap from the middle of verse 1 to the middle of verse 3. Perhaps one reason the structure omits this is because it is biographical, not doctrinal, as is the rest of the structure. There are other places we must consider as well. We will take out of consideration verses 11 and 15, which have been discussed previously and are therefore accounted for in the analysis but in verses 27 and 28, there appears to be a blank spot with seemingly important and doctrinally relevant information. I confess that this spot does not fit the larger chiastic structure, from what I can tell. Welch's chiasm in Alma

36 has similar struggles.[155] Although I have no explanation, it is interesting to note that this space forms another compelling chiastic structure:

> A And they are free to <u>choose liberty and eternal life</u>,
> > B through the <u>great Mediator</u> of all men,
> > > C or to choose <u>captivity and death</u>,
> > > C' according to the <u>captivity and power</u> of the devil;
> > B' I would that ye <u>should look to the great Mediator</u>,
> A' be faithful unto his words, and <u>choose eternal life</u>

Dominance

A convincing analysis must account for and embrace the dominant nouns, verbs, and distinctive phrases in the text. Conversely, a weak construction relies upon relatively insubstantial or common words and ideas in the text. Accordingly, powerful chiastic structures revolve around major incidents, unique phrases, or focal words, as distinguished from insignificant or dispensable parts of speech.

The structure in 2 Nephi 2 employs dominant nouns and verbs with very distinct words and phrases such as: "Redeemer," "Messiah," "salvation," "redeemer," "salvation is free," "good from evil," "the law," "grace and truth," "presence of God," "intercession

---

155 Welch's Alma 36 has these problems too. Take, for example, the phrase "born of God." It occurs four times in this passage (and seven times in the book of Alma). Two of these occurrences are worked into the chiastic structure by Welch: verses 5 and 24. A third occurrence, in verse 26, can also be worked into the structure, because it occurs between elements L and J. The fourth occurrence, in verse 23, is found between elements M and L. If, as Welch asserts, this passage were deliberately intended to be chiastic, why would the author include elements that break the structure? A similar problem afflicts element I, which is actually misplaced in the chiastic structure. Again, to labor the point, the phrase "harrowed up" occurs three times (verse 12, 17 and 19). Two of these, verse 17 and 19, can be worked into the chiastic structure. The third, in verse 12, cannot. These anomalies, however, have not persuaded other serious scholars to reject Welch's structure.

for all," "opposition," "creation," "eternal purposes," "act nor to be acted upon," "Adam," "Garden of Eden," "children," and "prolonged" (lengthened). Interestingly, the word "opposition" occurs only seven times in the LDS standard works: once in 1 Timothy 6:20, once in Doctrine and Covenants "Official Declaration" 1:15, once in Joseph Smith—History 1:20; and four times in the Book of Mormon, all of them in 2 Nephi 2. It should be noted that only in 2 Nephi 2 is the word "opposition" used in a doctrinal context. Similarly, the word "intercession" occurs only fifteen times in all of scripture, with only four occurrences in the Book of Mormon, two of them being found in 2 Nephi 2. The other two occurrences in the Book of Mormon are found in the Book of Mosiah (chapters 14 and 15) where Abinadi quotes or paraphrases Isaiah 53. The word "intercession" is clearly rare and, once again, as used in 2 Nephi 2, appears strictly in a doctrinal context. Even the word "act" is rare; being found just fourteen times in the Book of Mormon, with eight of those being located in 2 Nephi 2— and always used in a doctrinal context.[156]

Mavericks

A chiasm loses potency when key elements in the system appear extraneously outside the proposed structure. The analyst is open to the charge of selectively picking and choosing among the occurrences of this element if some of its occurrences in the text are arbitrarily ignored.

There is no issue on this point with perhaps one exception. The proposed structure leaves out a small yet seemingly important phrase located in verse 15: "And to bring about his eternal purposes in the end of man, after he had created our first parents, and the beasts of the field and the fowls of the air, and in fine, all things which are created, it must needs be that there was an opposition; *even the forbidden fruit in opposition to*

---

156 The same doctrinal usage of the word "act" can also be found in Alma 12, which, as will be demonstrated later in the chapter, also contains a chiasm similar in structure and doctrinal content to that of 2 Nephi 2.

the tree of life; the one being sweet and the other bitter." The items of interest here are the different fruits. One is the forbidden fruit, obviously from the tree of knowledge of good and evil; the other, though not explicitly stated, is the fruit of the tree of life. At first glance there is a textual logic that would seem to indicate that the forbidden fruit is the one being referred to as "sweet" since it is mentioned first and then so described in a parallel the latter part of the sentence. Similarly, the fruit of the tree of life would appear to be, according to the text, the one that is "bitter" for the same reasons. However, there is another possible meaning. When viewed from a chiastic perspective, the fruit of tree of life could be the one that is sweet, while the forbidden fruit would be bitter. This latter perspective would seem to concord with Lehi's description in 1 Nephi 8, where the fruit of the tree of life is described by Lehi as being "most sweet, above all that I ever before tasted. Yea, and I beheld that the fruit thereof was white, to exceed all the whiteness that I had ever seen. And as I partook of the fruit thereof it filled my soul with exceedingly great joy." Additionally, he states that "it was desirable above all other fruit." (1 Nephi 8:10–12) This symbolic tree and its associated fruit appears to be not only the same tree as described in the Garden of Eden story but also the same as described in Alma's discourse (see Alma 32) wherein the tree and the fruit are depicted in similar fashion: "The fruit thereof, which is most precious, which is sweet above all that is sweet, and which is white above all that is white, yea, and pure above all that is pure" (Alma 32:42).[157]

Centrality

The crux of a chiasm is generally its central turning point. Without a well-defined centerpiece or distinct crossing effect, there is little reason for seeing chiasmus. Inverting is the essence of chiasmus, so

---

157 For more information on this see C. Robert Line, "Bitter and Sweet: Dual Dimensions of the Tree of Life," *Sperry Symposium 2011*, Deseret Book.

the clearer the reversal at the center point, the stronger the chiasticity of the passage.

The chiasm here, in whole, contains over thirty-two separate and chiastically corresponding elements, the main chiastic structure being represented as follows:

A Jacob, <u>I speak unto you</u>; Thou art my first born <u>in the days of my tribulation</u> (v. 1)

B thou art redeemed because of the righteousness of thy Redeemer: he cometh to bring salvation unto men (v. 3)

C He shall <u>minister in the flesh</u> (v. 4)

D For the <u>spirit is the same</u> (v.4)

E <u>the way is prepared</u> from the fall of man (v. 4)

F and <u>salvation is free</u> (v. 4)

G instructed sufficiently that they <u>know good from evil</u>. By the <u>law they are cut off</u> (v.5)

H <u>redemption</u> cometh

I in and through the Holy <u>Messiah</u> (v.6)

J **The Atonement (v.6-10) Christ atonement makes possible eternal life— spiritual rebirth**

K there is an opposition/with sweet and bitter examples (v.11)

L must needs have been (v.12)

M created for a thing of naught (v.12)

N the end of its creation (v.12)

O the wisdom of God, and his eternal purposes (v.12)

P1 if there is no God, we are not, neither the earth:

P2 for there could have been no creation of things

P3 neither to act

P4 nor to be acted upon (v.13)

Q wherefore, all things must have vanished away (v.13)

P1' there is a God

P2' and he hath created all things

P3' both things to act,

P4' and things to be acted upon (v.14)

O' to bring about his eternal purposes
(v. 15)

N' in the end of man, after that he created
our first parents (v.15)

M' all things which are created (v.15)

L' it must needs be (v.15)

K' there was an opposition/with sweet and bitter
fruits (v.15)

**J' The Fall (18-25) Adam fall makes mortality
possible— physical birth**

I' <u>Messiah</u> cometh in the fulness of time,

H' that he might <u>redeem</u> the children of men from the
fall (v.26)

G' they are free forever <u>knowing good from evil</u>; . . . save
it be by <u>the punishment of law</u> (v.26)

F' Wherefore, <u>men are free</u> according to the flesh;

E' <u>all things are given them which are expedient unto man</u> (v.27)

D' the will of <u>his Holy Spirit</u> (v.28)

C' according to the <u>will of the flesh</u> (v.29)

B' which giveth the spirit of the Devil power to captivate, to bring
you down to hell (v.29)

A' I <u>have spoken these few words unto you all</u>, my sons, <u>in the last
days of my probation</u> (v.30)

The two smaller chiasms are not only well balanced but both contain vital doctrinal teachings of the gospel, mainly, the Fall and the Atonement:

J1 he is full of grace and truth. . . . offereth himself . . . to answer the ends of the law (v.6–7)
  J2 no flesh that can dwell in the presence of God (v.8)
   J3 resurrection of the dead, being the first that should rise (v.8)
    J4 he shall make intercession for all the children of men (v.9)
     J5 they that believe in him, shall be saved (v.9)
    J4' because of the intercession for all (v.10)
   J3' all men cometh unto God
  J2' they stand in the presence of Him (v.10)
J1' the truth and holiness which is in him. Wherefore, the ends of the law (v.10)

J6 an angel of God . . . had fallen . . . wherefore he became a devil (v.17)
  J7 knowing good and evil (v.18)
   J8 after Adam and Eve had partaken . . . they were driven out of the garden of Eden (v.19)
     J9 the family of all the earth (v.20)
      J10 the children of men
        J11 days . . . were prolonged, according to the will of God (v.21)
          J12 that they might repent while in the flesh (v.21)
        J11' their time was lengthened, according to the commandments which the Lord God gave (v.21)
      J10' the children of men (v.21)
     J9' all men . . . were lost (v.21)
   J8' if Adam had not transgressed . . . he would have remained in the garden of Eden (v.22)
  J7' doing no good, for they knew no sin (v.23)
J6' Adam fell that men might be . . . men are that they might have joy (v.25)

In each case the center point of each chiasm (the Fall, the Atonement, and the main chiasm) focuses on uniquely important concepts, each of which is doctrinally interrelated to the other:

The Fall: Men are lost because of transgression
The Atonement: Christ makes intercession for all
Main Chiasm: Opposition in all things; otherwise
there is no creation nor existence

Elder Nelson and Elder McConkie have both taught that
these three doctrinal pillars, the Creation, the Fall, and the
Atonement are the three core elements of the plan of salvation
and are doctrinally interrelated. Without the Fall, which creates
the opposition needed to make progress, and without the
Atonement, which creates the reconciliation necessary to realize
progress, there could be no existence. This doctrinal aspect of the
center point of the chiasm as a whole in 2 Nephi 2 finds similar
support in the center point of the following chiasm in 2 Nephi
11:6–7, which interestingly contains the words of Nephi, perhaps
quoting or paraphrasing the words of his brother Jacob:[158]

A that save Christ should come all men must perish
  B For if there be no Christ
    C There be no God
      D And if there be no God we are not
      D For there could have been no creation
    C But there is a God
  B And he is Christ
A and he cometh in the fulness of his own time

There are two necessary realities for a meaningful and
purpose-driven existence: the Fall and the Atonement. Inherent
in both the Fall and the Atonement is the God-given gift of
agency. People have to be able to choose, "To act for themselves,"
but there also has to be the possibility of redemption provided
through the Atonement if people make wrong choices. In 2
Nephi 11:6–7, and in 2 Nephi 2 (by implication) we see that

158 See David E. Sloan, *Journal of Book of Mormon Studies: Volume 6, Issue 2*, Pages: 67—98; Provo, Utah: Maxwell Institute, 1997.

the Atonement is a necessary element for existence to be, as it is a counterbalance, a response, or a solution to the Fall. As the effects of the Fall came about through the application of agency, so also do the divine effects of the Atonement come about only when agency is employed.

Both of these chiastic centers (the Fall and the Atonement) also bear a doctrinal likeness to the following passage found in D&C 93, which contains the other reality upon which existence rests, mainly choice, or agency: "Man was also in the beginning with God. Intelligence, or the light of truth, was not created or made, neither indeed can be. All truth is independent in that sphere in which God has placed it, to act for itself, as all intelligence also; otherwise there is no existence" (D&C 93:29-30). Thus the chiasm in 2 Nephi 2 contains both elements, and both elements are the central focus of the chiasm. Such an occurrence, with regard to Welch's criteria of *centrality*, is a strong indication of intentional chiastic structure.

Furthermore, such chiastic structures within greater structures (such as we see here in 2 Nephi 2) are not uncommon in the Bible, especially in a text (for example) that Lehi would certainly have known, studied, and was very familiar with in the brass plates. One such example is the text found in Genesis 32:1-33:20.[159] Similarly, Nigel Turner suggests that 1 Corinthians 5:2-6 is a chiasmus within a chiasmus.[160]

Reduplication

If the same word or element appears over and over within the system, the likelihood is greater that some other kind of repetition (including random repetition) is predominant in the passage instead of chiasmus.

The proposed chiastic structure in 2 Nephi 2 passes well on this point. There is hardly any extraneous repetition at all, which

---

159 See Appendix 1.

160 In *A Grammar of the New Testament*, vol. 3: Syntax [Edinburgh: T. & T. Clark, 1963]

adds considerable weight to it being an intentional composition when one considers the multitude of elements contained therein, not to mention their uniqueness and originality as discussed previously.

Balance

How balanced is the proposed chiasm? Ideally, the elements on both sides of the proposed focal point should be nearly equal, in terms of number of words, lines, or elements. It reduces clarity and focus when the two halves of a purportedly chiastic passage are not balanced.

The chiasm in 2 Nephi 2 has good (almost precise) balance, with 731 (49.8 %) words in the first half and 737 (50.2 %) words in the second, which makes this chiastic structure slightly more balanced than the chiasm in Alma 36. Elements within the overall chiasm, as well as the two smaller chiasms, are perfectly balanced, with each smaller chiasm appearing opposite of the other and related to each other doctrinally (the Fall and the Atonement), bound also by the center point of the main chiastic structure.

Climax

A strong chiasm will emphasize the central element of the passage as its focal climax. Where the concept at the center is not weighty enough to support the concentrated attention of the reader and to bear the author's paramount intention, the chiastic force of the passage is less than the case in which the idea at the center is an important one.

In this case, the climax is definitely significant and purposeful. The doctrinal center of the chiasm exhibits beauty, form, and content: the need for opposition in all things (including the Fall and the Atonement), the veracity of creation, the existence of God and His eternal purposes, the absolute requisite of agency, and the reality of existence. These elements interestingly, contribute to and form the basis of a fascinating philosophical and metaphysical reality. A few things should be noted as it relates to this particular point of criteria. The central crux of Lehi's chiasm could be seen in some ways as a tacit rejection of the French existentialist philosopher Jean-Paul Sartre, who maintained that human beings have no essence before their existence because there is no Creator. Thus, as he stated, "Existence precedes essence."[161] In contrast, Lehi would argue the opposite: essence defines existence. If there were no Creator, there would be no existence. Sartre would argue that we exist first and determine our essence by means of choice. Lehi would say that choice is a fundamental necessity for there to be existence. Consequently, essence, in reality, precedes existence, and man is entirely subject to God's plan, or "eternal purpose."

Return

A chiasm is more complete where its beginning and end combine to create a strong sense of return and completion. Second in importance to the central crossing effect in a lengthy chiasm is the way the chiasm begins and ends. The overall structure becomes more apparent when the boundaries are clearly defined and where the passage begins and ends similarly.

The return on the Lehi chiasmus in 2 Nephi 2 is remarkable. Notice the beauty and relationship of the beginning and the end: "Jacob, I speak unto you; Thou art my first born in the days of my tribulation (v.1)" and "I have spoken these few words unto you all, my sons, in the last days of my probation (v.30). The components are unmistakably symmetrical. The beginning and ending also employ themes that Lehi will later use to develop the center, or crux, of the chiasm, including freedom to choose (agency, see v. 4-5 and vv. 26-27), the Fall (v. 4 and 26), and redemption (vv. 3, 6 and 28).

Compatibility

The chiasticity of a passage is greater when it works comfortably and consistently together with the overall style of the author. Chiasm is

---

161 *Existentialism and Humanism,* 27

more likely to be meaningfully present if its author used chiasmus or related forms of parallelism on other occasions as well. If a proposed chiastic word order is an isolated phenomenon in the writings of an author, there is a greater chance that the occurrence in question was simply accidental.

Is there evidence of chiasmus in any of Lehi's other writings as preserved in the Book of Mormon? Interestingly, like Alma's counsel to his sons (Helaman in Alma 36 and Corianton in Alma 42), Lehi's counsel to his sons, sons-in-law, and "adopted" son is very much chiastic. His counsel also falls squarely within the "boundaries" rule. According to Welch, "Whenever one reads a text, especially a text with ancient origins, one ought to be mindful of the text's division into segments or units, and that chiasmus afforded a seriously needed element of internal organization in ancient writing."[162]

The following is an interesting series of Lehi's words as recorded by Nephi, all in a section of 2 Nephi wherein Lehi is giving counsel to the next generation. As will be seen, these structures, although not of the magnitude and doctrinal elegance of 2 Nephi 2, lend weight to the argument that Lehi used chiasmus in other instances; in fact, in apparently the very same venue we find in 2 Nephi 2: counsel to posterity through the chiastic medium. Such repeated occurrence and context, as we shall see, strongly indicates that the proposed structure in 2 Nephi 2 is hardly an isolated phenomenon or linguist fluke. For our purposes (and for the sake of brevity), I will leave an in-depth analysis of these structures to a future study. The suggested chiastic structure I present here will suffice for my present purposes.

---

162   John W. Welch, "What Does Chiasmus in the Book of Mormon Prove?" in *Book of Mormon Authorship Revisited: The Evidence for Ancient Origins*, ed. Noel B. Reynolds (Provo, Utah: FARMS, 1997), 205. Welch also writes that "the design and depth of the Book of Mormon often comes to light only when the book is studied with chiastic and other ancient literary principles in mind," ibid., 222.

2 Nephi 1:4–22 (Lehi to Nephi's brothers)

A Jerusalem destroyed (v.4)
  B Land of liberty; cursed shall be the land (v.7)
    C Keep commandments, prosper in the land (v.9)
      D They shall dwell safely forever (v.9)
        E Received great blessings from the Lord (v.10)
          F They reject the Holy One of Israel (v.10)
            G Scattered and smitten (v.11)
              H Bloodsheds and great visitations (v.12)
                I Would that ye would remember (v.12)
                  J Awake, awake from a deep sleep (v.13)
                    K Shake off chains by which ye are bound (v.13)
                    K' Which are the chains which bind the children of men (v.13)
                  J' Awake! And arise from the dust (v.14)
                I' Desire that ye should remember (v.16)
              H' Fulness of Gods wrath upon you (v.17)
            G' Cut off and destroyed (v.17)
          F' Led according to will and captivity of the devil (v.18)
        E' Choice and favored people of the Lord (v.19)
      D' His ways are righteous forever (v.19)
    C' Keep commandments, prosper in the land (v.20)
  B' Not come into captivity; cursed with sore cursing (v.21-22)
A' Eternal destruction (v.22)[163]

---

163 Subsequently there is a transition in the text (v. 23), and even though he still continues his counsel to Nephi's brothers, there is another chiastic structure, one that reinforces and summarizes the first.

2 Nephi 1:24–27

A Nephi's views have been glorious (v.24)

  B Nephi has kept the commandments (v.24)

    C Ye have sought to take away his life (v.24)

      D You accuse him that he has sought for power and authority over you (v.25)

        D' He hath not sought for power and authority over you (v.25)

      C' He (Nephi) has sought the glory of God and your eternal welfare (v.25)

    B' Manifest boldly concerning your iniquities (v.26)

A' Spirit of the Lord upon Nephi, opened his mouth to utterance that he could not shut it (v.27)

2 Nephi 1:28–29 (Counsel to Laman and others)

A And now my son, Laman, and also Lemuel and Sam . . . also the sons of Ishmael (v.28)

  B If ye hearken I will leave my first blessing (v.28)

  B' If ye will not hearken I take away my first blessing (v.29)

A' Nephi (implied in v.29 at the end)

2 Nephi 1:30–32 (Counsel to Zoram)

A Thou art the servant of Laban (v.30)

  B brought out of the land (v.30)

    C Thou hast been faithful (v.31)

      D Long prosperity upon the face of this land (v.31)

        X Nothing save it shall be iniquity shall harm or disturb (v.31)

      D' Prosperity upon the face of this land forever (v.31)

    C' If ye keep the commandments (v.32)

  B' consecrated this land (v.32)

A' Security of thy seed with the seed of my son (v.32)

2 Nephi 3:1–25 (Lehi to his son Joseph)

A I speak unto you Joseph, my last-born (v.1)

 B In the days of my greatest sorrow did thy mother bear thee (v.1)

  C thy seed with thy brethren (v.2)

   D thy seed shall not utterly be destroyed (v.3)

    E covenants of the Lord which he made unto Joseph (v.4)

     F fruit of his loins (v.5)

      G bringing them out of darkness into the light, yea, out of hidden darkness (v.5)

       H a choice seer will I raise up out of the fruit of thy loins (v.6-7)

        I He shall do none other work, save that which I command (v.8)

         J Moses will I raise up (v.10)

          K a seer will I raise up (v.11)

           L I will give [the seer] power to bring forth my word (v.11)

            M not only bring forth my word, but convincing of word (11)

             N Fruit of thy loins shall write (v.12)

              O fruit of loins of Judah shall write (v.12)

             N' written by the fruit of thy loins (v.12)

              O' written by the fruit of the loins of Judah (v.12)

             M' to confound false doctrines, contentions, make peace (12)

            L' Out of weakness [the seer] shall be made strong (v.13)

           K' That seer will the Lord bless (v.14)

          J' I will raise up a Moses (v.17)

         I' Yet I will not loose his tongue that he shall speak much (v.17)

        H' I will raise up [a seer] unto the fruit of thy loins (v.18)

       G' they shall cry from the dust (v.20)

      F' fruit of thy loins (v.21)

     E' covenant which I made unto thy fathers (v.21)

D' thy seed shall not be destroyed (v.23)

  C' the seed of thy brethren (v.24)

B' Remember the words of thy dying father (v.25)

A' Blessed art thou Joseph, thou art little (v.25)

2 Nephi 4:4–7(Sons and daughters of Laman)

A inasmuch as ye shall keep my commandments ye shall prosper in the land (v.4)

  B inasmuch as ye will not keep my commandments ye shall be cut off from my presence (v.4)

    C But behold, my sons and my daughters (v.5)

      D I cannot go down to my grave save I should leave a blessing upon you (v.5)

        X if ye are brought up in the way ye should go ye will not depart from it (v.5)

      D' I leave my blessing upon you (v.6)

    C' upon the heads of your parents (v.6)

  B' wherefore, because of my blessing the Lord God will not suffer that ye shall perish (v.7)

A' wherefore, he will be merciful unto you and unto your seed forever (v.7)

2 Nephi 4:11 (Lehi to Sam)

A blessed art thou

  B and thy seed

    C thou shalt inherit the land like unto thy brother Nephi

      D and thy seed

        X shall be numbered

      D' with his seed

    C' thou shalt be even like unto thy brother

  B' thy seed

A' thou shalt be blessed in all thy days

The structures presented above are sufficiently simple and plain enough to strongly suggest that Lehi, at least as recorded by Nephi, was disposed to employ chiastic structures.[164]

Aesthetics

Finally, there is room for subjective appreciation. Computers alone cannot identify chiasmus. Since human readers must judge an author's artistic success, further factors become relevant in assessing a passage's degree of chiasticity, such as the author's fluency with the form; consistency in sustaining the structure, balance, and harmony; pliability at the turning point (which yet does not draw undue attention to itself); and meaningful applications of the form that do not resort to subtleties so obscure as to be esoteric or awkward.

2 Nephi 2 is an elegant chiasm because it employs two chiasms within the main chiasm— the two smaller ones contain important material that adds to the main doctrinal components of the Fall and the Atonement and are aligned within the larger chiasm opposite each other in a poetic parallel. Furthermore, as has been stated, the form and content are a nice fit in Lehi's chiasm. The use of antithetical parallelism specifically is compelling and powerful as it fits the content and context of "opposition in all things," with the Fall and the Atonement being doctrinally connected to each other (i.e., one gives meaning to and is in essence defined, in context of the other).

---

164 One thing of note: Nephi seems to cover the bases well when giving the firsthand chronicling of his father's counsel to all these different groups and peoples, with one exception: himself! Nephi doesn't record his father's words to him. We would assume Lehi would give counsel to all. Maybe it was too sacred for Nephi to record? Maybe what Lehi said to Nephi couldn't be said in front of the others because it would cause too much contention? Maybe Lehi didn't give him counsel because he didn't need it? In the beginning of the Book of Mormon, Lehi does the same thing with Laman and Lemuel and compares them to valleys and rivers but doesn't compare Nephi with anything, probably because he doesn't need the counseling and encouragement to improve his behavior.

Historical Relevancy and Potential Sociolinguistic Connections

Why is the presence of chiasmus in the Book of Mormon important? Simply put, the claim is made both implicitly and explicitly that the book is of ancient Semitic origin; therefore, if so demonstrated, it should be considered not only an historic text but likewise religiously relevant. The fact that the Book of Mormon contains multiple examples of this Middle Eastern linguistic structure in no way proves its authenticity with certainty, yet it posits the book in a light which makes it difficult dismiss it as simple fiction. Likewise, the book's highly aesthetic and poetic structure precludes such a technique from being ascribed solely to chance. Although not all interested observers are convinced, there seems to be a growing number of scholars both within and out of the LDS church who are fascinated and even perplexed with the existence of chiasmus, to the degree that the bona fide presence of chiasmus is summarily conceded.

However, it may be worthwhile to examine this phenomenon from a different perspective and inquire as to the historical transmission of the chiastic form throughout the extant time line of the Book of Mormon. This is to say that chiasmus, if genuine, would most likely not have haphazard or unconnected occurrences scattered randomly throughout the book. Take, for instance, what is widely considered the best example of and most well-known chiastic structure, located in Alma 36. Did Alma the Younger unwittingly happen upon this chiastic form by chance with no prior knowledge of what other writers had composed? This is possible but not very probable. Did he discover it by himself by reading the scriptural accounts as contained in the brass plates handed down from generation to generation? Again, this is possible, but is it likely? What if there was another possibility? What if the chiastic form was passed through the various record keepers of the Book of Mormon who had been trained, tutored, and learned the form from previous record keepers? Is there a genesis and subsequent historical transmission of the chiastic form, and are there sociolinguistic and even doctrinal markers that could substantiate such an occurrence? It is my contention that there is and that the Book of Mormon contains in its pages the direct evidence of the form and the transmission thereof.

In some respects we would most likely expect chiasmus from the earlier writers in the Book of Mormon, especially Lehi and Nephi, since they were directly from Semitic lands and cultures, learned in all language (1 Nephi 1), and thus not far removed from the historical and artistic origins and impetus of Old Testament chiasticity. Additionally, the principle of entropy would tell us that chiasticity in the Book of Mormon, especially if we are laying claim to the Semitic-origin theory, would be less likely the further removed Nephite writers are from Lehi's advent to the land of promise. Such a notion might call into question the plausible authenticity of the Alma 36 chiasmus. Such a linguistically artistic albeit isolated compositional megalith, would seem to be more random than revolutionary, more indiscriminant than incredible, and more accidental than authentic.

What then, might be the relationship between Lehi's grand chiasm in 2 Nephi 2 and Alma's chiasmus in Alma 36? For one thing, both are massive in size, elegant, doctrinally dense, and have closely related center points. The sheer size and content alone of Lehi's chiasmus lends considerable weight to the plausible intentionality and authenticity of Alma's structure. In a sense they are doctrinal and pedagogical mirrors of each other; they both witness, substantiate, and validate each other as intentional and purposeful colossal structures. Perhaps another underpinning of the connective bridge can also be seen in other significant chiastic texts given by Alma himself and directly related to his chiasmus in Alma 36. After we establish and examine two of these structures, we will then contemplate the relationship they share with Lehi's chiasmus in 2 Nephi 2.

Alma 41 (Alma's Counsel to his son Corianton)

A I have somewhat to say concerning the restoration of which has been spoken (v.1)

 B that all things should be restored to their proper order (v.2)

  C judged according to their works (v.3)

   D restored unto that which is good (v.3)

    E restored unto them for evil (v.4)

     F all things shall be restored to their proper order, everything to its natural frame (v.4)

      G inherit the kingdom of God (v.4)

       H one raised to happiness according to his desires of happiness (v.5)

        I If he hath repented of his sins (v.6)

        J These are they that are redeemed of the Lord (v.7)

        K endless night of darkness (v.7)

        L thus they stand or fall (v.7)

        M they are their own judges (v.7)

        L whether to do good or do evil (v.7)

        K decrees of God are unalterable (v.8)

        J whosoever will may walk therein and be saved (v.8)

        I which ye have hitherto risked to commit sin (v.9)

       H Behold, I say unto you, wickedness never was happiness (v.10)

      G they are without God (v.11)

     F thing of a natural state and place it in an unnatural state . . . in a state opposite to its nature? (v.12)

    E but the meaning of the word restoration is to bring back again evil for evil (v.13)

   D mercy restored unto you again; ye shall have justice restored unto you again (v.14)

  C have a righteous judgment restored unto you again (v.14)

 B that which ye do send out shall return unto you again, and be restored (v.15)

A therefore, the word restoration more fully condemneth the sinner, and justifieth him not at all (v.16)

Alma 42 (Alma's Counsel to His Son Corianton)

A my son, I perceive there is somewhat more which doth worry your mind . . . concerning the justice of God (v.1)

 B time granted unto man to repent (v.4)

  C cut off from the tree of life (v.6)

   D subjects to follow after their own will (v.7)

    E no means to reclaim men . . . which man had brought upon himself because of his own disobedience (v.12)

     F the plan of redemption could not be brought about, only on conditions of repentance (v.13)

      G Now the work of justice could not be destroyed; if so, God would cease to be God (v.13)

       H all mankind were fallen (v.14)

        I they were in the grasp of justice (v.14)

        J cut off from his presence (v.14)

         K repentance granted (v.22)

          L mercy claimeth (v.22)

           M cease to be God (v.22)

           M But God ceaseth not to be God (v.23)

          L mercy claimeth the penitent (v.23)

         K because of the atonement (v.23)

        J bringeth back men into the presence of God (v.23)

        I law and justice (v.23)

       H mercy claimeth all (v.24)

      G can rob justice? I say unto you, Nay; not one whit. If so, God would cease to be God (v.25)

     F God bringeth about his great and eternal purposes, prepared from the foundation of the world (v.26)

    E thus cometh about the salvation and the redemption of men, and also their destruction and misery (v.26)

   D whosoever will come may come (v.27)

  C partake of the waters of life freely (v.27)

 B If he has desired to do evil, and has not repented in his days (v.28)

A O my son, I desire that ye should deny the justice of God no more (v.30)

It is not my intention to use Welch's criteria to fully assess the two foregoing structures; however, it appears they pass the criteria with flying colors. The only problem or exception with any of the specific points of criteria would be the balance issue in Alma 42, where there seems to be a gap between verses 17 to 21; however, upon closer examination, we notice a smaller chiastic interlude; in fact, it is doctrinal and beautiful in its poetic flair:

A how could a man repent
  B except he should sin?
    C How could he sin
      D if there was no law?
        E How could there be a law
          F save there was a punishment?
          F Now, there was a punishment affixed,
        E and a just law given,
      D Now, if there was no law given . . . if there was no law
    C given against sin
  B men would not be afraid to sin.
A or mercy either, for they would have no claim upon the creature?

Several points of interest are readily apparent when we consider these chiasms in light of Alma 36. First and foremost is size and doctrinal compatibility. Both chiasms (Alma 41 and 42) focus on core doctrine, especially the Fall and the Atonement. Here, then, is another connection with Lehi's chiasm in 2 Nephi 2: doctrinal density, sheer size, and significant doctrinal center points. For example, notice the relationship with Alma 42 and 2 Nephi 2 with regards to their center points: both focus on the reality of existence: "God would cease to be God" (Alma 42)/"all things would vanish away" (2 Nephi 2). Interestingly, the center points in these two chiasms (Alma and Lehi) also correlate (as previously discussed) with Nephi's doctrinal chiasm in 2 Nephi 11:6–7: "if there be no God we are not, for there could have been no creation." Such an occurrence seems highly unlikely. Is it possible? Perhaps statistically, but to ascribe this to a coincidence would appear to be highly untenable.

It is also interesting to note that Alma's grand chiasm in Alma 36, along with those just mentioned in Alma 41–42, are similar to Lehi's in that they contain counsel to their sons. As we have demonstrated, Alma and Lehi gave counsel via chiasmus not just to one but to multiple sons (see Alma 36, 41, and 42; cf. 2 Nephi 1–4). Thus given all these correlates, the likelihood of Alma 36 being a text with intentional structure becomes even more probable because it follows a doctrinal, historical, and even genealogical pattern! One wonders if Lehi's counsel to his sons in 2 Nephi 1–4 served as a template for Alma in constructing the beautifully crafted chiastic counsel for his sons in Alma 36–42. It seems highly reasonable. It could be said that Lehi's Chiasm in 2 Nephi 2 profoundly influenced Nephi's structure in 2 Nephi 11:6–7 and that both influenced Alma.

Here we might also mention another significant and interesting chiastic structure composed by Alma the Younger (Alma 12) that correlates, like Alma 42, with Lehi's chiasmus in 2 Nephi 2.

Alma 12

A he that will harden his heart, the same receiveth the lesser portion of the word (v. 10)

 B he that will not harden his heart, to him is given the greater portion of the word (v. 10)

  C his glory, and in his power, and in his might, majesty, and dominion (v. 15)

   D he is merciful unto the children of men, and that he has all power to save (v. 15)

    E second death, which is a spiritual death; (v. 16)

     F captivity of Satan, he having subjected them according to his will (v. 17)

      G as though there had been no redemption made; for they cannot be redeemed (v. 18)

       H if it had been possible for Adam to have partaken of the fruit of the tree of life the word would have been void, making God a liar (v. 23)

I And we see that death comes upon mankind, (v. 24)

    J1 there was a space granted unto man in which he might repent (v. 24)

        J2 therefore this life became a probationary state (v. 24)

        J3 a time to prepare to meet God (v. 24)

        J4 a time to prepare for that endless state (v. 24)

    I plan of redemption . . . shall bring to pass the resurrection of the dead, (v. 25)

    H if it were possible that our first parents could . . . partaken of the tree of life plan . . . frustrated . . . word of God would have been void, taking none effect. (v. 26)

   G made known unto them the plan of redemption, (v. 30)

  F being placed in a state to act according to their wills (v. 31)

 E second death, which was an everlasting death (v. 32)

 D for on such the plan of redemption could have no power, (v. 32)

C supreme goodness of God. (v. 32)

B If ye will repent and harden not your hearts, then will I have mercy upon you (v. 33)

A whosoever will harden his heart and will do iniquity, . . . he shall not enter into my rest. (v. 35)

Why mention chiasmus in Alma 12? Despite the fact that this chiasm seems to be isolated from Alma 36 and 41–42, it also supports the claim that Alma not only knew of and used the chiastic form but used it with purpose. Alma's chiasm in Alma 12 is reminiscent of the structure previously demonstrated in Alma 42 in that both chiasms are similar in size and doctrinal makeup. Both chiasms reference not only the Garden of Eden story but the specific symbolic imagery of "cherubim and a flaming sword," which is only mentioned twice in the entire Book of Mormon, both in doctrinal chiasms of Alma the Younger. Furthermore, the notion of "acting for oneself" is encountered again in a rare doctrinal usage, reminiscent, once again, of Lehi's chiasm in 2 Nephi 2. Alma the younger, it would appear, borrows these doctrinal phrases as teaching devices in his own writings. The influence of Lehi on Alma would appear almost certain, since there are really no linguistic correlates anywhere in the Book of Mormon that approach these constructions.

There is also another salient issue to consider with regard to Alma's chiasticity. In the case of Alma 36, and 41–42, the form appears to be linked to genealogical and doctrinal considerations. Here in Alma 12, though, the author seems to also use it for rhetorical and doctrinal reasons. First, consider his audience. Zeezrom, a lawyer who "was the foremost to accuse Amulek and Alma, he being one of the most expert among them," (Alma 10:31) and also one Antionah, a chief ruler (see Alma 12:20). Alma may have tried to appeal to their academic and logical leanings by teaching doctrine by the power of the Spirit, accompanied and facilitated by the intellectually persuasive and artistic form of chiasmus (see Alma 12:20). Alma would probably have related easily to Zeezrom, perhaps because he was once like him— learned but lacking the Sprit (see Alma 11:21). Apparently Alma's design worked on both levels, since Zeezrom was intellectually astonished (see Alma 11:46; cf.14:6) and spiritually convicted, for he "began to tremble" (Alma 11:46). Later, Zeezrom "began to tremble more exceedingly, for he was convinced more and more of the power of God; and he was also convinced that Alma and Amulek had a knowledge of him, for he was convinced that they knew the thoughts and intents of his heart; for power was given unto them that they might know of these things according to the spirit of prophecy" (Alma 12:7). Could it be that Alma's ability to teach the word both by spiritual power and intellectual persuasion was the key to Zeezrom's miraculous and intense conversion? It could well be, for Alma, we remember, was a man "of a sound understanding and [he] had searched the scriptures diligently, that [he] might know the word of God. But this is not all; [he] had given [himself] to much prayer, and fasting; therefore [he] had the spirit of prophecy, and the spirit of revelation, and when [he] taught, [he] taught with power and authority of God" (Alma 17:2–3).

It would seem plausible that if Alma the Younger used chiasmus, so would his father, Alma. However, at present we do have any record of such chiastic composition. Is this, then, a weak link? It should be remembered that absence of evidence is not evidence of absence. Perhaps we do not have any record because Alma the Elder was not a record keeper, but Alma the Younger was; having received the record directly from King Mosiah (see Mosiah 28:20). However, one wonders if Alma taught the form to his son. This is plausible since Alma the Elder would have been learned in the scriptures; in fact, when he was a priest to Noah, he was likely only academically learned.[165] He didn't become spiritually converted until Abinadi touched his heart. Perhaps this is one of the reasons Alma the Younger rebelled. Maybe, prior to his father's conversion, he had seen in his father religious form without spiritual substance, which perhaps contributed to his rebellion against and rejection of the Church.

---

165 It stands to reason that Alma the Elder would have this artistic train-ing because he was a priest of Noah and was learned in the law of Moses, even more so, he and they didn't obey it, therefore, they were probably more caught up in form than substance. In fact, his discourse in Alma 12 is a tacit self-indictment of his behavior in Mosiah 12—learning with-out living the scriptures. "For he put down all the priests that had been consecrated by his father, and consecrated new ones in their stead, such as were lifted up in the pride of their hearts. Yea, and thus they were sup-ported in their laziness, and in their idolatry, and in their whoredoms, by the taxes which king Noah had put upon his people; thus did the people labor exceedingly to support iniquity. Yea, and they also became idola-trous, because they were deceived by the vain and flattering words of the king and priests; for they did speak flattering things unto them" (Mosiah 11:5–7). It is conceivable that Alma the Elder also taught and influenced his son with regard to the doctrinal concept of hardening one's heart: "Now the eyes of the people were blinded; therefore they hardened their hearts against the words of Abinadi, and they sought from that time for-ward to take him. And king Noah hardened his heart against the word of the Lord, and he did not repent of his evil doings" (Mosiah 11:29). Alma the Younger picks up on this and warns the people thus in Alma 12 (see verses 9–11; see also Mosiah 13:11 and 17:2–4).

So far we have looked at an isolated group of individual Nephite record keepers, and we have seen some potential yet intriguing connections between their various chiastic writings. If we go a step further, however, we see that the interconnectedness grows greater when we consider the entire group of record keepers from Lehi to Alma the Younger. Let's first consider a simple list that documents the records keepers and the flow of records, at least from what we know through the Book of Mormon:

1. Lehi
2. Nephi (son of Lehi)
3. Jacob (brother of Nephi)
4. Enos (son of Jacob)
5. Jarom (son of Enos)
6. Omni (son of Jarom)
7. Amaron (son of Omni)
8. Chemish (brother of Amaron)
9. Abinadom (son of Chemish)
10. Amaleki (son of Abinadom)
11. King Benjamin (son of Mosiah I)
12. Mosiah II (son of Benjamin)
13. Alma II (son of Alma the Elder)

Thus far we have firmly established the likelihood that Lehi used chiastic writing in a doctrinal vein. We have established the same plausibility with Alma II and have demonstrated a relationship between him and Lehi with regard to several fascinating doctrinal and compositional connections. We also established earlier in the paper a similar connection with Lehi and Nephi, thus cementing the likelihood of that relationship through chiasmus.[166]

But what about the other aforementioned record keepers of the Book of Mormon? Are there similar chiastic connections and doctrinal markers we can trace through each of their

166 See, David E. Sloan, *Journal of Book of Mormon Studies: Volume 6, Issue 2*, Provo, Utah: Maxwell Institute, 1997, 67-98.

writings? For our purposes we cannot give an exhaustive list of evidence; however, perhaps a few relevant examples will suffice. We know that Lehi's younger son Jacob was a righteous man, a prolific teacher, and, very much admired and even quoted by his older brother Nephi. Here is one example that certainly appears chiastic (notice the midpoint of the chiasm. Again it is Jesus Christ):

Jacob 4:14–18

A because they desired it God hath done it, that they may stumble. (v. 14)

  B now I, Jacob, am led on by the Spirit (v. 15)

    C unto prophesying (v. 15)

      D Jews they will reject the stone (v. 15)

        E build and have safe foundation (v. 15)

          F this stone shall become the great, and the last, and the only sure foundation (v.16)

        E rejected the sure foundation (v. 17)

      D can ever build upon it, that it may become the head of their corner? (v. 17)

    C I will unfold this mystery unto you (v. 18)

  B my firmness in the Spirit (v. 18)

A and stumble because of my over anxiety for you (v. 18)

After Jacob we encounter a series of records keepers whose writings are small and essentially historical in nature: Enos, Jarom, Omni, Chemish, Abinadom, and Amaleki. With such limited space and perhaps lacking spiritual motivation,[167] we obviously would not expect much chiastic structure, especially chiasms that are doctrinal in nature. However, two intriguing examples do appear, and, interestingly, they both occur at the

---

167 "And as these plates are small, and as these things are written for the intent of the benefit of our brethren the Lamanites, wherefore, it must needs be that I write a little; but I shall not write the things of my prophesying, nor of my revelations. For what could I write more than my fathers have written? For have not they revealed the plan of salvation? I say unto you, Yea; and this sufficeth me" (Jarom 1:2).

end of each writer's record and are both doctrinal in nature, each centering on Christ and the Atonement.

Enos 1:26–27

A I saw that I must soon go down to my grave
 B I have declared it in all my days
  C and have rejoiced in it above that of the world
   D I soon go to the place of my rest
    E which is with my Redeemer
   D I know that in him I shall rest
  C I rejoice
 B in the day
A when my mortal shall put on immortality, and shall stand before him; then shall I see his face with pleasure

Enos thus ends his record with not only a powerful testimony of the Redeemer but an aesthetically pleasing testimony as well. The other record keeper is Amaleki. Although not technically chiastic, we nevertheless can see that even Amaleki, who penned only 19 verses, employed a beautifully poetic and artistic style as he also bore fervent testimony of the Savior as he concludes his record. This form is not only doctrinal in nature, but when his historic commentary is taken away from the lone 19 verses, this is all that remains, and how powerful it is both in spirit and form:

Amaleki (Omni 1:25–26)

A exhorting all men to come unto God
 B the Holy One of Israel
  C and believe in prophesying, and in revelations, and in the ministering of angels
A I would that ye should come unto Christ
 B who is the Holy One of Israel
  C and partake of his salvation, and the power of his redemption
A yea, come unto him
  C and offer your whole souls as an offering unto him

Element C is particularly intriguing in that it has a logic flow with regard to our spiritual development: believe, partake, and offer . . . this is to say one must first believe and have faith; then we must partake, or feast, on God's word through scripture, prayer, and worship; then we must offer, which is to say we then (and only then) can truly give something to the Lord and to our fellowman. Marlin K. Jensen once said that spiritual guidance cannot come from the spiritually weak. "When though art converted, strengthen thy brethren." It is with this beautiful form that the small plates of Nephi are filled and thus finished. From this point on the plates pass for the first time in the Book of Mormon out of the familial line and into the hands of King Benjamin, son of Mosiah I. King Benjamin apparently was familiar with and used chiasmus as well, with structures touching on the core doctrines of the Fall and the Atonement, just like his predecessors. The follow examples will suffice:[168]

Mosiah 3:18–19

(Men will drink damnation to their souls unless)
(a) They HUMBLE themselves
  (b) and become as little CHILDREN
    (c) believing that salvation is in the ATONING BLOOD OF CHRIST;
      (d) for the NATURAL MAN
       (e) is an enemy of GOD
        (f) and HAS BEEN from the fall of Adam
        (f') and WILL BE forever and ever
       (e') unless he yieldeth to the HOLY SPIRIT
      (d') and putteth off the NATURAL MAN
     (c') and becometh a saint through the ATONEMENT OF CHRIST
    (b') and becometh as a CHILD
   (a') submissive, meek and HUMBLE.

---

168 http://www.jefflindsay.com/chiasmus.shtml

Mosiah 5:10–12

(a) And now it shall come to pass, that whosoever shall not take upon him the NAME of Christ

(b) must be CALLED by some other name;

(c) therefore, he findeth himself on the LEFT HAND of God.

(d) And I would that ye should REMEMBER also, that this is the NAME

(e) that I said I should give unto you that never should be BLOTTED out,

(f) except it be through TRANSGRESSION;

(f') therefore, take heed that ye do not TRANSGRESS,

(e') that the name be not BLOTTED OUT of your hearts.

(d') I say unto you, I would that ye should REMEMBER to retain the NAME

(c') written always in your hearts, that ye are not found on the LEFT HAND of God,

(b') but that ye hear and know the voice by which ye shall be CALLED,

(a') and also, the NAME by which he shall call you.

It has been suggested that the use of parallelism in this passage emphasizes the danger of transgression (sin) and the importance of remembering the name we are to take upon us—Christ. Thus it appears that King Benjamin received his knowledge from his Nephite forefathers, and like they did, he passed this knowledge on to his sons, including Mosiah II:

> And it came to pass that he had three sons; and he called their names Mosiah, and Helorum, and Helaman. *And he caused that they should be taught in all the language of his fathers*, that thereby they might become men of understanding; and *that they might know concerning the prophecies which had been spoken by the mouths of their fathers*, which

were delivered them by the hand of the Lord. And he also *taught them concerning the records which were engraven on the plates of brass*, saying: My sons, I would that ye should remember that were it not for these plates, which contain these records and these commandments, *we must have suffered in ignorance*, even at this present time, not knowing the mysteries of God. For it were not possible that our father, Lehi, could have remembered all these things, to have taught them to his children, except it were for the help of these plates; for he having *been taught in the language of the Egyptians* therefore he could read these engravings, and teach them to his children, that thereby they could teach them to their children, and so fulfilling the commandments of God, even down to this present time. . . . O my sons, I would that ye should remember that these sayings are true, and also that *these records are true*. And behold, also the plates of Nephi, which contain the records and the sayings of our fathers from the time they left Jerusalem until now, and they are true; and *we can know of their surety because we have them before our eyes*. And now, my sons, I would that ye should remember to *search them diligently, that ye may profit thereby*; . . . And many more things did king Benjamin teach his sons, which are not written in this book" (Mosiah 1:2-8; emphasis added).

We do not have many of the direct writings or first-person quotations from Mosiah II, but what we do have is amazing, especially in Mosiah 29. Mosiah II chiasmus is even more likely because this example was thought out and written down: "Therefore king Mosiah sent again among the people; yea, even a written word sent he among the people. And these were the words that were written, saying" (Mosiah 29:4):

Mosiah 29:5–32

A I desire that ye should consider the cause which ye are called to consider—for ye are desirous to have a king (v.5)

 B which would cause him and also this people to commit much sin (v.9)

 C let us be wise and look forward to these things, and do that which will make for the peace of this people (v.10)

  D let us appoint judges, to judge . . . according to our law . . . according to the commandments of God (v.11)

  E if it were [to] have just men . . . it would be expedient that ye should always have kings (v.13)

   F whosoever has committed iniquity, him have I punished

    G according to the law which has been given by fathers (v.14–15)

     H For behold, how much iniquity doth one wicked king cause to be committed,

      I yea, and what great destruction!

      J Yea, remember king Noah, his wickedness and his abominations

       K And were it not for the interposition of their all-wise Creator,

        L because of their sincere repentance,

         M they must unavoidably remain in bondage

         N but he did deliver them

          O because they did humble themselves before him

          O because they cried mightily unto him

         N he did deliver them

         M out of bondage

        L extending the arm of mercy towards them

       K that put their trust in him (v.19-20)

      J ye cannot dethrone an iniquitous king

      I through much contention, and the shedding of much blood. . . . he teareth up the laws

H and he trampleth under his feet the commandments of God (v.21-22)

　G he (a wicked king) enacteth laws . . . after the manner of his own wickedness;

　　F and whosoever doth not obey his laws he causeth to be destroyed;

　　　E thus an unrighteous king doth pervert the ways of all righteousness (v.23)

　　　　D choose you . . . judges, that ye may be judged according to the laws . . . given you . . . by the hand of the Lord (v.25)

　　　　　C this shall ye observe and make it your law—to do your business by the voice of the people (v.26,29)

　　　　　　B the sins of many people have been caused by the iniquities of their kings (v.30-31)

A I desire that this inequality should be no more in this land, . . . I desire that this land be a land of liberty (v.32)

Once again, notice that the midpoint (K through O) deals with Christ and the Atonement: *trust him, repentance, mercy, deliverance, bondage,* and *humility.* This is particularly poignant because these words and phrases are contained in only one verse, which phrases (and verse) are unique in comparison to the rest of the chiasm.

Apart from the smaller writers mentioned previously, whose intention it was apparently to simply pass on the plates, we see evidence that a continuous doctrinal chain of chiastic form exists from Father Lehi, on through each record keeper, and ultimately to Alma the Younger. It would indeed be interesting to determine in future studies if a chiastic/doctrinal connection exists among the succeeding record keepers of the Book of Mormon after Alma II. This would be especially intriguing since the scope of writing/record keeping seems to change after Alma 42 to a more narrative based and historical style. Although the message of the gospel of Christ is continuously taught throughout the remainder of the book, the megalithic doctrinal discourses on the Atonement seem to dissipate from this point on.

Conclusion

In the multitudinous step pyramids of Mesoamerica[169] reminiscent of the ancient ziggurats of Mesopotamia,[170] whose highest point was the place of holiness, sacrifice, and atonement, we can see a doctrinal model that likewise applies to the poetic steps and structure of the beautifully handcrafted and divinely inspired chiastic writings of the Book of Mormon. The center points of these chiastic structures in the Book of Mormon are likewise of sacred and holy significance. Just as the step pyramid allowed an individual to access the holy presence, so likewise do the chistocentric chiasms of the Book of Mormon allow the reader to access Him in who all things center, even Jesus Christ. It should be clear from the abundance of chiastic witnesses in the Book of Mormon, including that of Lehi in 2 Nephi 2, that Book of Mormon writers, including and especially Nephi and Lehi, labored "diligently to write, to persuade our children, and also our brethren, to believe in Christ, and to be reconciled to God" (2 Nephi 25:23). Nephi also declared that "the fulness of mine intent is that I may persuade men to come unto the God of Abraham, and the God of Isaac, and the God of Jacob, and be saved" (1 Nephi 6:4).

Interestingly, Nephi says in 2 Nephi 11:4 that he delights not just in the truth of the Atonement (i.e., the coming of Christ) but in "proving" it! One might wonder why the Book of Mormon had to be preserved on plates. Why couldn't Joseph Smith receive it directly from revelation? Perhaps it is because of a sort of chiastic code that needed to be transmitted. "Wherefore, the Lord hath commanded me to make these plates for a wise purpose in him, which purpose I know not" (1 Nephi 9:5). Often we say the wise purpose was to serve as a duplicate record because the Book of Lehi would later be lost. However, is it possible that the wise

---

169 Cholula, Chichen Itza, Teotihuacan, Xochicalco, Uxmal, and El Tajin, to name a few. There are many more.

170 The top of ziggurats were symbolic of Gods presence.

purpose was also a linguistic code of sorts? "And now remember, my son, that God has entrusted you with these things, which are sacred, which he has kept sacred, and also which he will keep and preserve for a wise purpose in him, that he may show forth his power unto future generations" (Alma 37:14). Such a scriptural code, through chiastic style as a means of textual transmission, could be considered a type of scriptural encryption similar to parables, which veil and conceal doctrinal verities. It could well be that the form not only preserves the content, but it authenticates it as well. This is analogous to the practice of sealing a letter with wax; however, in this case it's much more effective and clever because it is encrypted. Interesting that the Lord says, "I will show unto the children of men that I am able to do mine own work." Apparently this could be the case on several fascinating levels (2 Nephi 27:21). Most of the record keepers end with a doctrinal chiasm testifying of the Atonement of Christ.

The chiastic structure in 2 Nephi 2 is a key link, demonstrating that Father Lehi not only was familiar with chiastic structure but that he employed it in a skillful and elegant way to teach the doctrines of eternity. He furthermore, as it should now be obvious, impacted his sons Nephi and Jacob in their writings and ultimately impacted others in the Book of Mormon such as Alma and Mormon. John Welch has surmised that "literary beauty was synonymous with form. Becoming so fluent in the use of a form that the form itself becomes almost invisible, or at least does not draw undue attention to itself, is the mark of a great artist."[171] As has been noted by Church leaders and chiastic scholars alike, the primary purpose of the Book of Mormon is to convince both Jew and gentile that Jesus is the Christ.[172] David E. Sloan has suggested that the "plainness of Nephi's testimony of Christ may be sufficient to attract the gentiles, but it will probably require the preciousness and

171 Welch, "What Does Chiasmus in the Book of Mormon Prove?" 206.
172 See 2 Nephi 26:12 and the title page of the Book of Mormon

beauty of his poetic writings to convince the Jews, who should recognize that he wrote according to the 'learning of the Jews' (1 Nephi 1:2) and after 'the manner of prophesying among the Jews' (2 Nephi 25:1).[173]

John Welch has stated: "Anyone who claims that a passage is chiastic should be able to prove it."[174] The chiastic structure of Lehi's counsel to his son Jacob in 2 Nephi 2 has been clearly demonstrated. The chiasm aligns well with all the criteria, both from an objective and aesthetic point of view. Along with Alma's chiasm in Alma 36, this chiasm ranks as one of the most elaborate of all chiasmus in all literature. As Welch would say, "It merits high acclaim and recognition. Despite its complexity, the meaning of the chapter is both simple and profound. [Lehi's] words are both inspired and inspiring, religious and literary, historical and timeless, clear yet complex—a text that deserves to be pondered for years to come."[175]

In whole, Lehi's chiasmus could be viewed as literary masterpiece whose doctrinal message and construction should be considered on par with the great chiasmus in Alma 36. In fact, given the length and complexity of the chiasm, its doctrinal nature, and its focus on the Atonement, it could well be that Alma drew inspiration to construct his chiasmus in Alma 36 based on Lehi's composition in 2 Nephi 2. Once again, the existence of this chiastic structure lends weight to Alma's and strongly suggests that neither could be the result of mere chance or coincidence.

---

173 David E. Sloan, *Journal of Book of Mormon Studies: Volume 6, Issue 2,* Pages: 67–98; Provo, Utah: Maxwell Institute, 1997.

174 John W. Welch, A Masterpiece: Alma 36, Provo, Utah: Maxwell Institute

175 Ibid.

Appendix 1

The overall literary arrangement of Genesis 32:1—33:20 ("Jacob Receives a New Name") is as follows:

A Jacob continues his journey to Canaan (1a)

  B The angels of God encounter Jacob and he names the place "two camps" (1b–2)

    C Jacob's embassy to Esau (3–6)

     D In fear Jacob prepares to meet Esau (7–21)

      E Jacob, his wives and children cross the Jabbok (22–23)

       X JACOB WRESTLES WITH A "MAN" AND HIS NAME IS CHANGED TO ISRAEL (24-32)

      E' Jacob prepares his wives and children to meet Esau (33:1–2)

     D' Jacob meets Esau and bows before him seven times (3)

    C' Jacob and Esau greet each other (4–7)

  B' Jacob explains his "two camps" to Esau, then they depart from one another (8–16)

A' Jacob arrives in Canaan (17–20)

I. Literary Arrangement of Genesis 32:1–32 ("Jacob at Jabbok, Israel at Peniel")

A Angels of God encounter Jacob, and then he renames the place "Mahanaim" (1–2)

    B Jacob sends messengers, listing his possessions to Esau (3–8)

        X JACOB'S PRAYER TO THE LORD (9–12)

    B' Jacob sends messengers and gifts to Esau (13–21)

A' A "man" opposes Jacob, blesses and changes his name to Israel, place is renamed "Peniel" (22–31)

A. Genesis 32:9–12. A chiastic substructure of Genesis 32:1–32. This is an expansion of "X" of Genesis 32:1–32.

Since this structure is a subset of a larger unit, all the letters are in lowercase.

The Literary Arrangement of Genesis 32:9–12 "Jacob's Prayer to the LORD"

Introduction: Jacob's invocation (9a)

a God's word to Jacob while in Haran (9b)

  b God's promise of prosperity to Jacob (9c)

    c Jacob's confession (10a)

      d Jacob left Canaan with only a staff (10b)

        x THE JORDAN RIVER: A PLACE OF CONTRAST (10c)

      d' Jacob returns to Canaan with "two camps" (10d)

    c' Jacob's petition (11)

  b' God's promise of prosperity to Jacob (12a)

a' God's word to Jacob while in Canaan (12b)

B. Genesis 32:22–32. A chiastic substructure
of Genesis 32:1–32

The Literary Arrangement of Genesis 32:22–32
"Jacob's Confrontation with God"

A Jacob did not cross the Jabbok at night but remained alone (22–24a)

  B A "man" wrestles with Jacob (24b–25)

   C The "man's request to Jacob (26a)

    D Jacob requests a blessing (26b)

     E The "man" asks Jacob his name (27a)

X JACOB'S NAME IS CHANGED FROM JACOB TO ISRAEL (27b–28)

     F' Jacob asks the "man" his name (29a–b)

    D' The "man" blesses Jacob (29c)

   C' Jacob's response by naming the place "Peniel" (30a)

  B' Jacob says he has seen God "face to face" (30b)

A' The sun rose upon Jacob as he crossed over Peniel [alone] (31)

II. Literary Arrangement of Genesis 33:1–20 ("Reconciliation: Jacob Returns Esau's Blessing")

A Jacob and Esau's greeting (1–7)

  B Esau's refusal of Jacob's present [minkah] (8–9)

   C Jacob's request of finding grace [hen] before Esau (10a)

    D Jacob asks Esau to take his present [minha] (10b)

X "I SEE YOUR FACE AS ONE SEES THE FACE OF GOD AND YOU HAVE RECEIVED ME GRACIOUSLY" (10c–d)

    D' Jacob requests Esau to take his blessing [berakah] (11a)

   C' God has dealt with Jacob graciously [hanan] (11b–c)

  B' Esau's acceptance of the present [object minkah omitted] (11d)

A' Jacob and Esau's departure from one another (12–16)

About the Author

C. ROBERT LINE HAS WORKED full-time with religious education for the past twenty-three years. In addition to teaching with the BYU Religious Education faculty, he has been a presenter at BYU Education Week, Women's Conference, and Especially for Youth, and has worked for CES programs as an instructor and director for Institutes of Religion.

Robert has both a bachelor's and master's degree from BYU and also holds a doctoral degree from Purdue University in Sociology of Religion. He has authored various books and articles and has served as the editor-in-chief of *Century Magazine*. Robert has served in the Church as a bishop, stake high councilor, elders quorum president, and various other callings. He played on the BYU men's basketball team from 1984 to 1985. He and his wife, Tamera Wright Line, have five children and four grandchildren. Their family resides in Cedar Hills, Utah.